INT
AFRICA

a personal journey

To Joe,
enjoy it + best wishes
Sept 30/2000

INTO AFRICA

a personal journey

YVONNE BLACKWOOD

Abbeyfield Publishers
2000 Toronto, Ontario

Canadian Cataloguing in Publication Data
Blackwood, Yvonne
Into Africa : a personal journey

Includes index. ISBN 0-9682274-9-X

1. Ghana – Social life and customs. 2. Nigeria - Social life and customs.
3. Blacks – Canada – Race identity. 4. Jamaican Canadians – Ethnic identity.
5. Blackwood, Yvonne – Journeys – Ghana.
6. Blackwood, Yvonne – Journeys – Nigeria.
I. Title.

DT510.4.B52 2000   966.705   C00-930926-8

Editing
Bill Belfontaine, Abbeyfield Consultants
Toronto, Ontario

Cover and textual design and layout
Karen Petherick, Intuitive Design International Ltd.
Markham, Ontario

Cover Photo
Digital Imagery® 1999, Photodisk, Inc.

Printed in Canada by TTP Tradeworx Ltd.,
Mississauga, Ontario

DEDICATION

In memory of dearest grandmother Eliza Williams,
the only mother I knew.

You taught me to give and not to expect to receive

To treat others with respect for respect will
be returned

To smile for it is contagious

To "study yuh book" for no one can touch
what's in my cranium

To make do with what I have

And most importantly, to love unconditionally.

"Twenty years from now you will be more disappointed
by the things that you didn't do than by the ones you did do.
So throw off the bowlines. Sail away from the safe harbour.
Catch the trade winds in your sails.
Explore. Dream. Discover."

~ Mark Twain

*N*o one knows the actual number, but it's stated (World Book) that twelve million black slaves were shipped from Africa to the western hemisphere. During the long, miserable journey nearly two million of them died. Over 60 percent of the survivors were brought to Brazil, Haiti, Cuba and Jamaica.

Although Africans had practised slavery since ancient times, most of those slaves were captured during wars and subsequently sold to Arab traders who came from northern Africa. Slave trade in the West Indies began with the Spanish after Christopher Columbus's journeys between 1492 and 1503, and continued when the British captured some of the Islands in the 1600's. During the 18th century, more than 600,000 blacks were brought to Jamaica to work on sugar, coffee and other plantations. It is therefore not a question of whether the mainly black population of Jamaica and the other West Indian Islands originated from Africa, but rather a question of which African countries they are from.

Born and raised in Jamaica, I grew up with my grandparents in Manchester, in the rural south central part of the island. Abiding by grandmother's teachings to "Learn yuh book," I excelled in elementary school and received a government scholarship to attend one of the best high schools in the Parish. Attending this bourgeois high school steered my life in a new direction. I was influenced in part by my teachers, mainly white Europeans and North Americans. But rubbing shoulders daily with the elites of the town, the children of doctors, lawyers, politicians and upper class business people, I soon learned to appreciate the finer things of life—fine dining, the arts, the theatre.

After graduating with flying colours, I left rural Jamaica for Kingston, the capital city. I worked for the Ministry of Education, my first job, then landed a job as audit clerk with the Royal Bank of Canada. Young and impatient, moving up the corporate ladder wasn't fast enough and after three years I quit to attend The College of Arts

Science and Technology where I majored in banking. I returned to the Royal Bank after graduation and landed a middle-management job. Life was good, my career was on an upward spiral. In the meantime, my fiancee who had emigrated to Canada to attend college, returned and we joined hearts then back to Canada he went! A year later after delaying to join him, I received a letter stating: "Join me in Canada now or else ..." Reluctantly, I left my beloved Jamaica to emigrate to colder climes.

In 1973, Jamaica had nationalized the Royal Bank of Canada, renaming it Royal Bank Jamaica Ltd. Because of this technicality a transfer was no longer available to employees and I had to resign and reapply in Canada.

After two months and unable to find a job of similar stature to the one I had in Jamaica, I joined the Royal Bank of Canada in Toronto as a teller. It took several years of hard work and many hours of studies at the University of Toronto and Ryerson Polytechnic Institute, to get back to management level. During those years, the horrible beast, racism, jumped up and licked my face like a playful puppy. It took me two years to realize what it was. But, I stand firm by my signature quotation, "Perseverance is a great element of success, if you knock long enough and loud enough at the gate, you are sure to wake up somebody." At the time of writing, I hold the position of Senior Account Manager Business Banking. My marriage ended after ten years.

I have no recollection of any discussion about slavery or Africa at home during my years in Jamaica. It was as if the subject was taboo. I had to rely on information from text books which were few and far between. But when my grandmother had all her grandchildren gathered around her on Sunday afternoons, story telling was our entertainment. During some of these storytelling gatherings I learned that grandmother's grandfather used to say, "I am Ashanti!" We knew it meant he was African, but we didn't know where in Africa he was born. That small bit of information stayed with me always.

Over the years as I learned the facts of life, and like an adopted daughter searching for her birth mother because of a compelling desire, so too I had a burning desire to see, feel, and touch the land of my forefathers.

Pregnant with desire, and an unshakable faith, I left Toronto during one of the coldest Januaries in fifty years, on January 11, 1997 on a journey to a land that I knew very little about and where I knew no one. The trip began on rocky ground as I had difficulty obtaining a visa for Nigeria and I left Toronto without one.

Many coincidences occurred and obstacles appeared that were resolved. The African men I encountered during the trip were amazing, their kindness overwhelming. It is said that nothing happens by chance or by good luck, that the people who came into our lives do so for a reason. Although I don't know it yet, I am convinced that in some way, the journey and one of these men will affect my life. Will it be Reverend Suobite—my guardian angel; the eccentric Professor Ojo; or Adamson, my driver, dinner companion, doctor? Who will it be? Only time will tell.

BLOCKADE!

$\mathcal{W}$ith six lengthy strides he arrived at the left side of the car, gun pointing at the driver's face.

"Who's in the car?" the soldier barked.

"Dis lady, is a sista visitin' from Canada," the driver said, pointing a nervous finger at me as I sat in the back seat of the old beat-up taxi. That didn't seem to be of any consequence to the soldier.

"Get out of the car!" he commanded. Slim built and handsome, he wore army fatigues with a black beret cocked to one side. "I say get out of the car, now!" he yelled.

As he spoke a gold tooth in the top row flashed like a firefly in a dark night. I was taken aback by his behaviour. It was coming on to dusk and we'd travelled for almost three hours along dusty Nigerian roads from Port Harcourt, heading for Owerri. We'd come upon several similar blockades manned by soldiers, but they'd waved us along pleasantly with a casual, "You're welcome," when the driver told them I was a Canadian tourist.

Before I had a chance to scoop up the contents of my makeup bag which was sprawled over my lap, the soldier pointed his gun at my head through the window. My God, the gun must have been at least five feet long! I froze. In one pulse of a heartbeat, I saw my brains splattered on the window at my right, small blobs of brain matter, matted with blood dripping onto the floor. Like melting ice cubes in a glass of rum, my body unfroze and my pupils focussed on the gun. I sprang from the car instantly, sending lipstick, powder and lip-liner tumbling onto the floor. All I could think of was, better be careful, don't make him angry and don't make him nervous. The driver, a pudgy, middle age man and Brother Tom, my escort, a medium built retired man, had jumped out of the car ahead of me with fear in their eyes.

"What you have in the trunk?" the soldier asked.

By this time the three of us were standing helplessly beside the car.

"My suitcase," I said in a low, feeble voice that escaped from my lips, scarcely believing it belonged to me.

"Open up the trunk," the soldier commanded and waved his gun menacingly.

My only thoughts at that moment were that this guy could learn some manners from the Canadian police. What about "please" and "ma'am" and all those pleasantries I'm accustomed to hearing? Even when they were being snarky and difficult, the Canadian police were always polite. "May I see your licence, ownership and insurance ma'am? Do you know you were doing a hundred and forty kilometres back there ma'am?" Those pullovers were annoying but nothing compared to this.

The driver quickly opened the trunk of the car, then stepped back to allow the soldier to look inside.

"Open it," he said brusquely, pointing his gun at the suitcase, then at me.

I opened my wallet, unzipped one of the compartments and fumbled through it to find the miniature key. Guns always made me nervous and having one pointed at me, caused ever heightening anxiety. In fact, I don't recall ever touching a real gun in my life. The closest I came to holding one was the time when my uncle-in-law accidentally shot himself in the finger while cleaning his revolver. At the time I lived with my aunt in Kingston, Jamaica and we were in the kitchen preparing the customary Saturday beef soup when an explosion rocked the house. I dashed toward the sound at the front of the house and was the first to arrive on the scene. Uncle was sitting in a basket chair on the enclosed verandah, dazed, while blood spurted from his index finger. The instrument of his folly, cold and mysterious, lay on the floor beside him. I thought of picking it up but changed my mind. I held uncle's hand until my aunt brought the first-aid-kit. Later I cleaned up the coagulated blood that was splattered across the glossy tiled floor.

Fully conscious of the Nigerian soldier and his gun, my hands shook while I tried to unlock the tiny padlock. Damn, I thought, I should've bought a bigger one. But who would've thought I would be opening my suitcase at the side of the road in the middle of nowhere? After a few moments, the key lined up in the minute hole. The lock snapped and I threw open the suitcase. The soldier proceeded to rummage through my clothing like a dog sniffing through garbage.

"I don't like to go through the lady's things, but I have to check," he said as he squeezed, pressed and poked my clothing.

Right! If he doesn't like to, why is he doing it? With great restraint, I held my tongue. I had nothing to hide, besides, I didn't want to provoke him. It seems he didn't find what he was looking for.

"Open your handbag," he ordered.

I opened the zipper and he peered inside but obviously he didn't see what he was looking for. A thick bundle of several thousands of nairas caught his eyes, but it seemed Nigerian money didn't interest him.

"Let me see what's in your wallet," he said.

At that moment I began to lose my temper. I smelled a rat and the stench was enough to make me gag. It seemed stories I'd heard about corruption and crookery in Nigeria were about to manifest themselves. Did this nincompoop think I was stupid that I couldn't figure out what he was up to? Thank goodness I travelled with little cash and had opted for mainly traveller's cheques.

"I thought you people were searching for guns and other weapons. What do you expect to find in my little wallet?" I asked with the innocence of a three-year-old child.

"Take out the money and give it to the driver to hold. I won't touch it."

He shifted the gun to his left hand, while he held up his right hand, palm upright. Although scared of the soldier and his weapon, I wanted to burst out laughing. Did he think not touching the money at that moment, made him honest? I removed all the money from the main compartment of my wallet, some nairas, fourteen hundred cedis (change left over from Ghana)and a fifty-dollar Canadian note. Several hundred American dollars, my only American cash, were tucked away in a side compartment of the wallet, but something told me not to show those, so he wasn't aware of them.

"Aha!" the soldier yelled with a victorious look on his face that said, now I have you. "You're importing currency into Nigeria. Do you know that is a federal offence?"

"You have got to be kidding!" I said boldly, knowing I'd done nothing wrong. It's amazing how a dose of self-confidence can help one overcome other emotions including fear. Suddenly the long gun no longer intimidated me. I realized the soldier was out of line.

"No, I'm not kidding," he mimicked me.

"The fifty Canadian dollar bill is for a taxi when I return home, and the cedis is change I got at the airport in Ghana when I bought a drink there. By the way, they're worth less than one United States dollar. I would like to know how you could call this importing currency," I said, pointing to the notes in my driver's hand.

"You're bringing in foreign currency into Nigeria. You should've changed it," he said adamantly.

"I know every country allows visitors small amounts of foreign currencies so don't give me that."

He ignored me and continued the charade.

"So what should I do with you?" he asked.

"Just let me go," I almost screamed at him. I felt the nerve endings in my head contract, cutting off the blood supply; a headache was imminent.

"What, with no punishment? Hi boss," he yelled to another soldier who sat in a folding chair on the other side of the road. "This lady is importing currency into Nigeria. I asked her what I should do with her and she said to let her go. What you think boss? What is a good punishment?"

As he led me across the road to the "boss," the word punishment resounded in my head, then like a bolt of lightening, it hit me. Damn you Yvonne, do you realize what you've done? Have you forgotten Nigeria is a military state, and not a democracy? How dare you mouth off to the soldier who is carrying out his masters' orders? Shivers began to race up and down my spine. My whole life flashed through my mind like data through a micro chip.

In the past, several stories had emerged about innocent people being tossed in Nigerian jails without bail. I thought about Ken Saro-Wiwa who was executed, and others who were thrown in jail without proper trials. What if the soldier decides to be nasty? What if he pins a charge on me? What if he butts me in the head with his gun, or shoots me. What if he throws me in jail? I doubted whether the driver and Brother Tom would stick their necks out and come to my rescue. The western world was up in arms about Nigeria and its human rights issues, but Sani Abacha, the leader, didn't seem to care. With Canada's withdrawal of its diplomats, it would've been difficult for me to get any justice.

I thought of my dear son waiting anxiously in Toronto for me to bring him back something from Africa. How would he react to the news that his mother was thrown in a Nigerian prison? I imagined my clients pointing fingers at me. "Why on earth did you go to Africa? Didn't you know it was dangerous?" I visualized my black friends who had encouraged me, calling up each other, "Did you hear the news? Yvonne is in prison in Nigeria. Let's pray for her." I visualized them running around trying to make influential contacts to help rescue me. The possibilities of my likely demise were daunting. Awash in a cold sweat, my tear glands opened fully. As hot, salty tears began to stream down my face, I prayed silently for mercy …

WHY AFRICA?

*T*here is an empty feeling of despair that one experiences when hopes and dreams are dashed, when control has been taken out of ones hands.

This was supposed to be a happy, exciting occasion, a trip of a life time. How did this vacation to West Africa disintegrate to such an impossible stage? How did a Senior Banker with a major Canadian Bank, end up on the dusty roads of Nigeria with two strangers and a soldier pointing a menacing gun at her head?

— ✧ —

A few weeks earlier, I'd been bragging to some of my clients about my proposed trip. At the time a Cheshire cat would've had difficulty competing with me.

"Why on earth would you choose to go to Africa of all places?" several of my clients and friends asked. I knew they were being polite, for the look on their faces and the tone in their voices said loud and clear, "Yvonne, you are nuts." I knew why they asked the question, for the continent of Africa was in an uproar in 1996.

In Niger, a military coup overthrew that country's first democratically elected President Mahamane Ousman, and placed him under house arrest. In Sierra Leone, Brigadier Julius Maado Bio ousted President Valentine Strasser in a bloodless coup. Rwanda also experienced a coup and horrifying massacres took place, with the Tutsi army held responsible. In Zaire, because of fighting between the Zairian army and the Tutsis, more than two hundred thousand Hutu refugees fled their refugee camps. Yes, I could understand the question. Africa at a glance, was no Club Med.

Despite all this 'doom and gloom', however, some positive things were happening in some parts of that continent. President Nelson Mandela signed the new definitive South African constitution enshrining the principles of multi-racialism and liberal democracy. In Liberia, Ruth Perry was elected as that country's first female Head of

State, and in Zimbabwe, President Robert Mugabe won the election with an uncontested vote.

"It's a long story, but one reason is my sister-in-law lives there," I answered simply.

If only they knew! There was so much more to the trip, but it would take a great deal of time and energy to also explain it to my white friends and clients, for them to get a full understanding of it. My deep desire and unquenchable feeling to visit "The Motherland" would have little meaning to them. To the few who could appreciate the continent of Africa, the response was, "Oh, you're going on a safari!" Little would they know that a safari did not feature in my agenda. To some of my black friends, the response wasn't encouraging, "Girl, you are brave. Aren't you afraid they'll kill you down there?" But for most of them, the response was, "You go girl!" They understood what it was all about. They were thrilled to have me as the ambassador charting the course, for none of them had visited the continent of their ancestry.

The trip was no following a will-o'-the-wisp, it stemmed from a childhood dream, a seed that was planted when I was a small child. It was nurtured and fertilized during my life, and like a fruit it ripened in 1996. A long gestation period you say? Yes, but nothing before its time, my grandmother Eliza used to say.

The seed was cast on fertile soil when I was about five years old. In those days, growing up in the tropical island of Jamaica, innocent and curious, story telling provided a popular pastime for we had no television. I heard the famous Ananse stories, our local folklore, over and over again. Ananse, always the cunning, crafty hero, tried to fleece everyone he encountered. In most of the stories, he succeeded. Not only did I hear those stories at home, I heard them at concerts and gatherings. The origins of those stories were never explained. One Sunday evening, in Canada, I attended a women's lodge function. A part of the evening's entertainment was story telling, and a plump, Ghanaian woman was the story teller. At a table surrounded by some of my girl friends, I listened keenly to what she said. When she told an Ananse story, the audience howled with laughter. Imagine my surprise when during the later mix-and-mingle session, I asked the story teller where the story originated. She said, "Ananse stories originated in Ghana." That surprised me, for not once did I hear Ghana mentioned at home in Jamaica.

My grandfather told all the grandchildren wacky duppy(ghost) stories. We would gather around him in the hall as the night shadows slowly took hold of the land. He told those stories vividly, and always so seriously, I couldn't tell if he made them up as he went along or if they were true. Actually, now that I think about it, I thought they were all true. My grandmother also told great stories, and they included ones about her grandfather. As one was recalled, the old man (grandmother's grandfather) had a vicious temper. When he became very angry, he would stutter, roll his eyes, thump his chest, and say, "I ... I am Ashanti!" That was supposed to put the fear of God in whoever was within listening distance. I knew it had something to do with Africa, but no one ever explained it. Those words resounded in my head for many years. Later, being old enough to understand it, I learned that great, great-grandfather garnered that information from his grandmother, who came directly from Africa.

This piece of information provided the only link to the Ashantis. In later years while studying geography and history I learned that the Ashantis were a tribe in Ghana, West Africa.

Jamaica's population of over two and a half million is mainly black. It is common knowledge that the blacks were kidnapped in West Africa—Ghana, Ivory Coast and Nigeria and brought to the island to work as slaves on plantations for the Spanish and later, the British masters in the sixteenth, seventeenth and eighteenth centuries.

The Spanish ruled the island after Christopher Columbus "discovered" it in 1494. The discovery was a standing joke with the Islanders, for the question always asked was, "How could Columbus discover a land that was richly populated by people—the Arawaks?" It wasn't long before most of the Arawaks were wiped out by European diseases that they had little immunity to, while others died from overwork.

After some gunplay, The British took control of Jamaica in 1655 making it a rich sugar plantation island. Finally, three hundred years later, Jamaica gained Independence on August 6, 1962, managing its own affairs since that time.

Little trace of slavery can be found on the island now, and I grew up there without hearing any discussions about slavery. Most of what I knew, I read in books. Jamaicans of the sixth, seventh, and generations beyond, are far removed from what transpired in the days of slavery.

The little information I'd learned about Africa, mainly from books, was of a general nature such as location, climate, names of popular politicians, and names of major tribes. Additional data came from both television and print media. Vivid pictures of starving, half-naked, poor people, with their faces painted, living in huts were already etched in my mind. Have you ever seen any rich Africans living a comfortable life style on any of the television programs? I can't recall. I knew they existed, and I wanted to see them for myself.

The nurturing of the idea to visit Africa began in the nineteen sixties when, as a teenager, I was fascinated by the American Civil Rights Movement. During that era, I learned about slavery in the United States, and heard how badly blacks were treated there. I heard about Dr. Martin Luther King Jnr., Rev. Jessie Jackson and others. That period saw a renaissance of blackness spread across America to the Caribbean like a wildfire. Many of us stopped straightening our hair and sported the popular Afro hairstyle. We resisted wearing makeup which was construed as trying to look white. I adored women like Nina Simone who sang Young, Gifted and Black, and Miriam Makeba who sang The Pata Pata Song. It was a time when many Caribbean people adopted African names, like Akilya, Akua and Kwasei. Black consciousness caught me in a web of wonderment about my ancestors. I realized some of them came from Ghana, but where else? How were they treated when they were plucked from their homeland? Were they princes and princesses, rich or poor, back in Africa?

I knew nothing about the history of blacks in Canada. The Underground Railroad, Harriot Tubman, and all the other black history stories, I learned about after making Canada my home.

In 1982, after living in Canada for six years, wrapped up in my own small world of family, home and work, I felt there had to be more to life than that. I became involved in community work. What an exposure that was! It was when I learned about the hardships and difficulties some blacks faced daily in their beloved adopted country. Racism was something I knew little about. In Jamaica my experience with prejudice was about social class, where servants couldn't dine with employers and gardeners had to enter houses through back doors. But I soon learned about its destructible power. I gained first hand knowledge of the difficulties encountered by people of colour and it stirred emotions I didn't know were simmering within me.

Fertilizing the idea took place later. I sat on a Four Level of Government Committee in 1992 to try to find solutions to address urgent issues in the black community in Toronto. This was immediately following a riot on Toronto's Yonge Street. It involved many youths, including some from the black community.

While I sat on the panel listening to deputations from young, black youths, pouring out their hearts and souls about their day-to-day encounters with racism, I too, cried. The tears slowly, involuntarily, slid down my cheeks. I carefully wiped them away under the guise of mopping my face.

Many times the cry of, "I don't know who I am," was expressed by the youths. They insisted that the contributions of African Canadians in the Canadian society must be addressed. They felt an alienation which made them reluctant to identify themselves as Canadian although many were born there. What saddened me most was the undertone of hopelessness. It reinforced and instilled in me the need to see the place of origin of black people. I asked myself then as I had done many times before, what was it about the land of Africa, that allowed its people to bear and withstand so much hardship, persecution, and suffering? What allowed them to be sold into slavery in the first place? I wouldn't find the answers in Canada, but would Africa tell me? No doubt many have asked the same questions and came up with rational answers or none at all. The thermostat of interest eased a few notches higher as the lure of Africa became stronger.

Travelling became a big part of my life over the years. I had a burning desire to visit many exciting places, to explore many things. I wanted to travel the world, to experience all the fascinating places I read about in history and geography books. (Of course the pocket book dictated how far I could go with that desire.) But most importantly, I wanted to be free to do it at my leisure. Having a real zest for adventure, these wonderful thoughts helped to nourish my mind. I tried to realize my dreams, and travelled the Caribbean extensively. I visited the Island of Bermuda, the furthest north (outside of the Caribbean chain)and travelled south visiting several Caribbean Islands along the way including St. Lucia, Grenada, to as far south as Trinidad, then on to touch the tip of South America when I visited Venezuela. I ventured across the Atlantic to Europe, and although these places were fun and exciting, another place kept beckoning to me.

An inexplicable, deep-rooted feeling remained with me constantly. Using the analogy of an adopted daughter bent on searching for her birth mother aptly described how I felt. I didn't know what to expect or what I would find, but I was willing to take the risk, for something more powerful than myself propelled me along. It was as if a part of me was missing. By finding it, I hoped it would make me more complete— if only in my mind. Whatever it was, I want to feel and experience a piece of it.

The idea of visiting Africa, wasn't with any great expectations of finding my roots. Although discovering one's roots had become very popular after Alex Haley's TV Mini series, Roots. There was no anticipation of making such a find, or discovering any long lost relatives, for I'd done no research toward that purpose. Armed with a smidgen of information that my great, great-grandfather was an Ashanti, I felt I had a link, however, and that made me feel that I would be accepted and welcomed in Ghana.

Just being in Africa, seeing the place, the people, feeling the air and smelling its unique scents, was all I wanted. Some African descendants experience this desire early and some later. Others feel the pull but hide from it. Some pretend they're not black, hiding behind terms like coloured and brown, while some do not identify with anything Afrocentric at all. Others experience it but circumstances prohibit them from pursuing it, circumstances such as family commitments and lack of money. Some in fact, never experience it. For me, something compelled me, and I knew I had to visit that continent before I died. I had to visit Africa while I was strong and healthy, I had to answer the call.

The ripening of the idea culminated when my previous sister-in-law, visited Canada in the autumn of 1996. I made up my mind that I could put it off no longer, I would make the trip to Africa.

VISA   OR   NO   VISA ?

*D*uring Joyce Ombede's visit to Canada in September 1996, we met several times. Although I'd divorced her brother several years prior, I remained good friends with her and all my previous in-laws. I occasionally visit her mother and father to see how they're doing and still take care of any banking business requiring attention. My philosophy is, if you didn't make it with your spouse, there's no need to hold malice for your in-laws, unless of course they were the reason for the marriage break down. And even at that, malice is a terrible emotion not worth harbouring. It eats away at you; forgiveness is better. Besides, if you had children with your spouse, the in-laws are, and always will be, the grandparents, aunts and uncles of your children.

Staying friendly and in touch has worked for me. It's worth the effort.

One evening I invited Joyce for dinner along with a few friends. Extricating my good china, crystal, and special flatware from the dark recesses of the buffet, I corralled my culinary skills and cooked dinner fit for a queen. My busy lifestyle rarely allows for these moments, but when time permits, hidden talents not only surprise my friends, but me, too. I could tell from the empty dishes and requests for recipes, that the hours spent preparing dinner were not in vain.

After the other guests departed, Joyce and I relaxed in the family room and while we sipped Drambuie, I broached the subject of my trip.

"So Joyce, I'm seriously considering coming to Africa. You know I've wanted to do this for several years, but keep putting it off. Every time there is a coup or fighting, I become apprehensive. I'm ready now. When is a good time to visit?"

"Oh Yvonne, that would be very nice," Joyce said, a hint of excitement in her singsong accent, "you must come during the dry season. January and February are good months."

Joyce's accent was unusual, for although she maintained her

native Jamaican enunciation, having lived in England, she'd acquired a slight British accent, too. This was now influenced by twenty years of living in Nigeria.

An unassuming woman, Joyce stood five feet, ten inches, and was as slender as a match stick. One finds it hard to accept that she mothered six children. She moved with a graceful sway, was always coordinated, with makeup expertly applied at all times. A quiet, humble person, she never elaborated on her education or her life in Nigeria. While studying in England she'd met Uche, a Nigerian student. They exchanged vows in the early nineteen seventies. Uche was no exception to what appears to be the Nigerian psyche— "They all eventually go home," and Uche returned to Nigeria with his Jamaican bride.

Uche, a brilliant man, is a professor and the Vice Chancellor of a large Nigerian university.

"I'll spend a week with you and your family. Hope that will be okay?" I asked.

"Of course. Uche and I would love to have you. We wouldn't dream of you staying in a hotel."

"Thanks, Joyce. I'll definitely take you up on it. I can't wait to see the children."

"You can well imagine how excited they'll be when I tell them someone is coming from Canada."

"I haven't been able to keep tabs on the children. Please write down their names and ages so I can bring them gifts that are appropriate."

Joyce had given birth to the children so fast, I couldn't keep track of their names, sex or ages.

She gave a haughty laugh, one that was unique to her. "Sure, I'll do it now before I forget. Do you realize my oldest is twenty already?" Joyce looked at me with the satisfaction of a proud mother. No doubt she'd fulfilled her husband's requirements.

"Really? It's hard to believe, but look at my son, he'll be seventeen next month. We're getting old."

"Speak for yourself!" Joyce laughed again. She was right. We didn't feel or look our ages. "Just let me know when you're coming. It's a little complicated to get to us. Here's my card with the address and phone number. When you get to Lagos, you'll have to take a domestic flight to Port Harcourt, and we will meet you there."

The card read: PROF. JOYCE OMBEDE, BA, MA, Ph.D, DEAN, FEDERAL UNIVERSITY OF NIGERIA.

"Why Joyce, I didn't know you are a Dean! And when did you get your Ph.D! How wonderful!"

I turned the card over, trying to absorb it all. How she found time to study and complete her doctorate while having all those babies was beyond me. Joyce laughed nonchalantly as she always does. She never explains anything. Life goes on as usual.

— ✧ —

Whenever I get together with some of my girlfriends(the sisters)to lime, a tete-a-tete, invariably we talk about relationships and difficulties with men. Sometimes the topic of discussions would be about West Indians and Black American women who marry native African men. Always a hot topic, voices would rise to a crescendo as each person vented her frustration or voiced strong views on the subject.

We heard stories about the African mother-in-law who made life extremely miserable for the foreign wife. In the end, many of these wives fled Africa, leaving behind their children and possessions to return to their native countries. There were also stories about how shocked some wives were when they arrived in Africa, only to realize that their husbands had two, sometimes as many as five other wives!

I sometimes wondered if Joyce experienced any of this, but was too embarrassed to talk about it. For me, these were stories because I had no proof that these situations existed or that any of them were true. I mean, I knew in the old days men had more than one wife, but I didn't think this was the case in modern Africa.

During the twenty years Joyce lived in Nigeria, none of her relatives had ever visited her. Over the years she'd sent photographs of her children to her parents, showing them at different stages of their lives, but the pictures were always professionally done and never candid shots.

Joyce's mother confided in me on many occasions about her concerns. On one of my visits we were sitting at the dining table in her small apartment. I was helping her to complete a small green withdrawal slip to be used to purchase a bank draft, when he turned to me, "Yvonne, I don't know how the hell my daughter survives in that

God forsaken place called Africa. Nobody knows anything about her life there. I don't know if the children have food to eat." She looked at me, bewildered. "And suppose she gets sick, what kind of care will she get? Another thing, she is scared of lizards. I know lizards are down there! I wish she would come back to Canada or America."

"Oh Mother B," I said, "you shouldn't worry so much. Joyce has visited you twice since she went to live in Africa, and she seems okay. Don't you think she'd say something if things were bad?"

"You don't know my daughter, she's so in love with her Uche, she wouldn't say a bad thing about him or his country."

There was no point arguing with her. Mother B was always emphatic about anything she discussed with me. She probably only wanted a listening ear. After that outburst I became deep in thought. Hmmm, I just wonder, there probably was an interesting story there ....

I didn't make any promises to my mother-in-law, but I made a mental promise to myself. I would find out what the real story was and put her mind at ease before she died.

When I said farewell to Joyce, the day before she left to return to Nigeria, I'd made a firm commitment that I would visit her in early 1997. I would contact her with a specific date and time of my arrival once it was finalized.

— ✧ —

In early December, I contacted a Travel Agency that specialized in trips to Africa to arrange a trip for me for the second week of January. That seemed an ideal time. Not only was it during the dry season as Joyce suggested, it was also just after the Christmas holidays. I always took a vacation at Christmas time, but changed it that year to allow my co-workers to have Christmas holidays instead. I was saddled with looking after two other jobs plus my own, a challenging feat, but I always loved a challenge. Sometimes I think I thrive on it! Whatever the masochistic satisfaction from the challenge, I couldn't wait to begin my vacation. Besides, escaping from the miserable cold winter to which I've never become accustomed, and which I dislike more with each passing year, was good medicine for me.

A few days before Christmas, Mohammed, my travel agent, called. I'd visited his office the day before to see how things were progressing. He was a Somalian with fine, chiselled features and a good physique. With Toronto being one of the most multicultural cities in the world,

I'd met a few Somalians. I'm yet to find one that is ugly, they're such beautiful people.

"Ms Blackwood, I've booked you to fly to Lagos, January 11 via Amsterdam, returning from Accra, Ghana, February 3 via Amsterdam," he said with a thick accent.

"That sounds fabulous, Mohammed. Thank you very much."

After he hung up, I stood in the middle of the kitchen staring into space. "Finally, I'm going to Africa!" I said aloud.

That night I couldn't wait to call my cousin in Rochester, New York. "Hi Peabody, I'm booked for Africa, leaving January eleventh."

"Hey, that's great. Don't forget to look up my church brother, Paddy, and take lots of pictures."

Peabody was a great traveller herself. She'd been all over the world, to places like Moscow and Egypt. We exchanged more pleasantries, then Peabody said, "By the way, did you get your visa for Ghana?"

"What visa? Do I need a visa for Ghana?"

"Yes, you do. Better check with your travel agent. Call me before you leave to let me know if everything is okay."

Early the next day, I called the agency.

"May I speak to Mohammed please?"

"Hold on," the voice at the other end of the telephone said.

I heard chatter in a language I didn't recognize, then a man came on the line.

"Hello, this is Mohammed, can I help you?"

"Mohammed, this is Yvonne Blackwood. You have me booked for a trip to Africa. Tell me something, do I need a visa for Ghana?"

"Oh yes," Mohammed replied, as if this was the most natural thing on earth.

"Do I need a visa for Nigeria, too?"

"Oh yes, you do."

"So when were you going to give me this information? You've booked my flight without telling me I need visas! What if I don't get the visas on time? What good will the flight be?"

At this point I was steaming with anger. My usual calm, quiet way of speaking eluded me. "What do I need to do to get these visas?" I snapped.

"I need your passport and three pictures plus twenty-three

dollars. I have application for Ghana visa. I'll send it off to Ottawa for you by courier. I will need extra twenty-five dollars for courier."

"How long will it take?"

"It usually takes two days, but with the Christmas holidays it may take a little longer."

"What about the visa for Nigeria?"

"Oh, they don't have embassy in Canada anymore. Canada severed diplomatic relations with them earlier this year."

"What!" I screamed.

I could sense Mohammed cringing through the phone as I tried to control my temper. He must have realized by then that I was the type who would not accept mediocre service.

I'd heard bits and pieces in the media about some human rights issues that involved Shell Oil in Nigeria, but hadn't paid much attention to the news. Now it seemed more serious than I thought.

"So how do I get a visa to Nigeria if they don't have an embassy here anymore?"

"I'll give you the phone number in the USA, and you can call to find out."

He sounded like a timid puppy. He gave me the Nigerian High Commissioner's office number in Washington. I wasted no time in calling the number.

"Hello, Nigerian High Commission. Can I help you?"

"Hello, I am calling from Toronto, and I'm trying to get a visa to visit Nigeria in two weeks time. Can you help me?" I felt desperate now. I hadn't bargained for this last minute glitch. Being organized is a vital element in my life. I hate to rush around the last minute.

"We do not issue visas here. This is the High Commissioner's office," a stern voice crackled through the phone. "You must contact the Consulate in New York. Here is the number."

I hung up, fuming.

"That travel agent is so blasted unprofessional," I swore under my breath. "What kind of service do they offer their clients? How can they be so bent on booking flights without making sure that people can travel? And to make matters worse, he doesn't know the difference between the High Commissioner's office and the Consulate!"

I called the New York number. There was a long exasperating recorded telephone message with many options. My temperature had reached the boiling point before I finally gathered that you must send an application along with your passport; a copy of your airline ticket; a photograph; twenty US dollars; a letter of invitation from your contact in Nigeria; copies of the first five pages of the contact's passport, and show means of support for yourself while in Nigeria.

With limited time to spare, I tried to contact Joyce in Nigeria to inform her that I needed a letter of invitation and copies of the first five pages of her passport. I soon learned that Nigeria is a difficult, if not impossible place to reach by telephone. I called from my office, I called from my home, I called late, I called early, but I couldn't connect with Joyce by phone. After five days of total frustration, I was at my wit's end. That night when I arrived at home, there was a message on my answering machine.

"Hello Yvonne, this is Reverend Father Davis from Nigeria; I'm here in Toronto. I'm a friend of Joyce Ombede, and she asked me to call you about your trip to Nigeria. I'm travelling back to Nigeria on New Year's Eve and hope we can travel together."

It was a voice I'd never heard before. His Nigerian accent was very pronounced but the tone was pleasant. Well, this is too much, I thought. It would be wonderful to travel with a priest, and a native Nigerian at that. He's safe, he knows the routine, he would be great company. But I didn't have a visa to travel to Nigeria. I returned Father Davis's call, but couldn't connect with him. He called me a second time and again we didn't connect. He left another message on my machine.

It was New Year's Eve when we finally connected.

"Sorry, we kept missing each other." Father Davis spoke with a soft, melodious voice. "I'm on my way to the airport and thought I would call you one more time."

"I'm so glad you were persistent. I'm desperate. I'm supposed to travel on January eleventh, but have no visa for Nigeria."

I gave him the information about the documents I needed from Joyce and implored him to deliver the message the moment he arrived in Nigeria. He promised he would, and I bade him bon voyage.

— ✧ —

Five days went by, and I heard nothing from Joyce. I called the Nigerian Consulate again to see what else could be done.

As I listened once more to the recorded message, I realized that I must submit the letter of invitation along with the passport pages or show means of support. I kept trying the number until I spoke directly to one of the counsels.

"What exactly do you mean by *means of support?*" I asked.

"You have to show that you have enough money to support yourself while you're in Nigeria," the man on the phone replied.

"How do you show the money?"

"You can send us copies of your travellers cheques."

"How much money is sufficient?"

"At least, US$100 per day for the duration of your trip."

"How long will it take to approve a visa?"

"Forty eight hours."

A warm feeling of relief spilled over me. I didn't have to sit around and wait for Joyce's letter and passport documents after all. I would just send copies of my travellers cheques, and the other required documents. Everything will be all right, I thought.

I had five days.

I picked up the telephone and dialled Ivor Farley, a good friend who lives in New York City.

"Ivor, my dear, I need you to do a favour for me."

"Oh yeah, what's that?" Ivor had a low raspy voice.

"I'm desperate ..."

"I know you'd come to your senses one day," Ivor cut in before I completed the sentence.

"It's not what you're thinking Ivor." I laughed then became serious again. "It's now January the sixth, and I'm supposed to travel to Nigeria on the eleventh. I'm planning to visit Nigeria and Ghana."

"All right man, yuh a go back to yuh roots!" he said, playfully in his native Jamaican accent.

"Listen Ivor, at this moment, I don't have a visa for Nigeria, but I have the documents required except an application form. Can you pick one up and fax it to me? I'll send you the completed form with the other documents by Federal Express. Can you take them in personally to the Nigerian Consulate in Manhattan?"

"Of course sweetie, you know you can ask me for a favour anytime." He reverted to his New York twang. "I'm on the afternoon shift, starting work at 3:00 p.m., so I can take it in first thing tomorrow morning. I'll pick up the application and fax it to you today. What's your fax number?"

Relief, blessed relief—I exhaled.

Ivor has been my good friend since the early nineteen seventies. I met him while dating my ex-husband. In those days, he was one of Bernard's best buddies. During my torrid romance with Bernard, we often double-dated with Ivor and his girl, Natalie. The four of us spent many nights at the Harbour View drive-in theatre, in Natalie's car. We partied together all over the city of Kingston, and other parts of Jamaica. Party animals, we were then. I remembered the warm nights when the gentle Trade Winds fanned our faces as we drove out to Port Royal, a thin peninsula which juts out from the south-eastern part of the island into the Caribbean sea. At this secluded enclave, once infested by Buccaneers and known as the wickedness city in the world, we bought sizzling fried fish and freshly baked cassava bammy from the women on the street. We would climb the wooden look-out-tower and sit inside the little house to eat our meal as we took a bird's eye view of the town. We spent some of the most enjoyable times of our lives together. Not once did Ivor make a pass at me during those years. We had a strong platonic relationship.

Ivor emigrated to the United States a few years after Bernard and I came to Canada, and for several years, we lost touch with each other. Ivor was never one to give up easily, and in the early nineteen eighties, he connected with us again. He never entered into holy matrimony during all these years, but he had a repertoire of several women, some of whom I met over the years. He also contributed his fair share to the children's population. Of medium height, and muscularly built, he had the most kissable lips, sort of like Teddy Pendergrass. I always wondered what they'd taste like. I was never sexually attracted to him, however, and always thought of him only as a good friend. He was handsome in a rugged sort of way with tight buns like some of those American football players. He continually talked as if he were a stud, but I always took what he said lightly.

In recent years, Ivor calls me sometimes on a Saturday or Sunday morning and tells me some of the most erotic things on the telephone.

"Ivor, you are the craziest man I know; please, stop saying these things," I would say as I blushed through the phone.

"A woman like you, you need a man to rub your head and massage ..."

I'd cut him off. "Ivor, forget it. I'm quite happy the way I am."

I think he gets his jollies from that sort of thing. Maybe he's trying to give me shock treatment? After the initial surprise of hearing Ivor talk dirty, I just laugh when he says some of these crazy things. I never take it seriously. More recently I've had a few lengthy discussions with him about the differences between men and women but they have been exasperating talks. No matter how hard I've tried, I've been unsuccessful with instilling one fact in Ivor's head—women like me, who are independent, self-sufficient and outgoing, can, and do survive quite nicely without having a man in their lives. In Ivor's warped mind, sex is the be-all and end-all of life. It is the thing that one lived and died for. If you're not having it, you can't be happy. How Ivor had become so one-track-minded was difficult to comprehend. I could bet my last dollar that he has never experienced happiness anywhere close to what I have, in years, and it has nothing to do with sex. This was a different Ivor, much different from the quiet, conservative young man I knew in the seventies. He'd become arrogant, impatient and mouthy. New York certainly affected him in a negative way. Well, I needed his help now, and I knew he would do anything in his power to help his friend.

While preparing the special Federal Express envelope with photocopies of the relevant documents for the Nigerian Consulate at my office, a fax arrived from Joyce with a letter of invitation and the first five pages of her passport.

Good Lord, what incredible timing!

I decided to include the faxed documents in the package although they weren't necessary. My thinking was, if Ivor goes to the consulate tomorrow, and it takes forty-eight hours to process, he can collect the visa and return it by Federal Express Friday, the tenth. It would be cutting it very close since my flight was scheduled for the eleventh, but I was confident everything would work out perfectly. After all, I was sending copies of traveller's cheques showing more than enough means of support plus Joyce's documents added extra ammunition. What could go wrong?

At noon the next day, I'd just given one of my clients the good news that his seven hundred and fifty-thousand dollar loan was approved. He was pleased and I was happy for him. It had taken some creativity to put his deal together, but it was worth the effort. This deal would help to put my month end figures into the stratosphere! I cradled the telephone in its holder and it rang immediately. I picked it up, expecting to hear Mr. May's voice asking another question.

"Hi Yvonne," Ivor growled. My ears pricked up immediately.

I didn't like the edge in his voice. The smile disappeared from my face immediately. "I don't think you're going to Nigeria this trip. The people at the Consulate turned down your application."

"What?" I barked before I could think. Calm down Blackwood, after all, Ivor is only the messenger. No need to yell at him. I lowered my voice. "What reason could they have to turn me down after all the documents I sent them?"

"I told them they were a flipping bunch of idiots. I told them they should be paying a woman like you, to visit their country. I told them no wonder their country is in such a bloody mess," Ivor swore angrily.

I knew Ivor was on my side and wanted to do what he could for me, but my heart sank lower and lower with every word he uttered. I'd hoped Ivor wouldn't take his arrogance to the Consulate. I knew those people in authority have a tendency to be vindictive.

"So what did they say?" I asked, trying my best to remain calm.

"They said Joyce can't send you an invitation letter because she's not a Nigerian citizen. The letter and the passport copies must come from her husband."

"Just imagine it. Joyce has lived for twenty years in that country, had her six children born there, is a university dean, and she can't invite someone to visit. Does that make sense?"

"Don't ask me," Ivor said.

"But what about the means of support? I sent copies of enough travellers cheques to show I can support myself while I'm in Nigeria. I should qualify without Joyce's documents."

"Look Yvonne, they refuse to give you the visa and there is nothing else I can do. I'll send you your stuff by FedEx this afternoon. Sorry sweetheart. You'll just have to make it a one-country trip and visit Ghana only, this time." Ivor sounded weary, and he was right, there was nothing more he could do.

"Thanks for all your trouble Ivor, just FedEx the documents for me. I'll see what else I can do from here."

I sat staring at an imaginary spot on my desk for several seconds after Ivor hung up. I fantasized that I could see that audacious son-of-a so-and-so who turned me down. I crushed his neck with my bare hands; it felt good. I returned to reality.

The information from Ivor was disheartening. It was too late to get new documents from Joyce's husband, plus it was extremely difficult to contact Nigeria by telephone. I'd planned the trip with Nigeria as the focal point intending to spend a week in Lagos and visit with Carlton Sewell. Carlton was the High Commissioner for Trinidad to Lagos. While visiting London a few years earlier, I'd met him when he was High Commissioner there. He'd been reassigned to Nigeria as that country's High Commissioner two years previously, and we'd corresponded up until two months ago. After visiting with Carlton, I'd planned to spend a week with Joyce in Owerri, and the final week in Ghana.

What can I do now? The grey matter in my head began to rotate like a ceiling fan at high speed. There must be a way. I haven't waited this long to have my plans go to ruin. This dream, this desire, this trip had taken me long enough to execute. It couldn't possibly bite the dust now. Slowly, as if hypnotized, I picked up the phone and dialled.

"Hello Mohammed, this is Yvonne Blackwood. Please change my flight to fly to Accra instead of Lagos. I didn't get the visa for Nigeria through the New York office. Do you think I'll have any problems getting it in Ghana?"

"Oh no, I think you should be able to get it from Ghana without any problem. By the way, you must bring in your ticket, and I'll replace it with a new one. It will cost twenty-five dollars."

Mohammed seemed to be more concerned with collecting his flipping twenty and twenty-five dollar fees, than with providing efficient service to his customers. If I had time, I would love to have taught him a thing or two about customer service. I'd show him how to go the extra mile and remind him that when you're in the service industry, you have no choice but to "kiss up" to your clients; no clients, no business.

Once I received my documents from Ivor I hurried to Mohammed's office to collect my new ticket in exchange for the old. He booked a flight for the same day as the original one to Nigeria, but this time I would travel from Toronto via Amsterdam to Accra, Ghana. The return flight would be the reverse.

"Say, Mohammed, once I get the Nigerian visa I would like to return from Lagos if that is possible. Can the return destination be changed once I'm in Nigeria? It would save me time and money instead of travelling back and forth from Nigeria to Ghana."

"Yes, you can change it. Just visit the KLM office in Lagos, and they'll change it. There's no charge as the fares for both destinations are the same." Why did I believe Mohammed?

ADAMSON

I stared out the tiny window, scant inches away from the aeroplane's right wing, as the KLM 747 touched down like a butterfly on a rose petal at Kotoka Airport in Accra, capital of Ghana. A burst of applause exploded from the passengers, and I applauded along with them, but not for the same reason as they did. I, Yvonne Blackwood, had arrived in the "Motherland." I'd finally realized a dream, reached a goal, achieved a desire planted like a seed since childhood. For that reason I applauded.

Moments later my feet touched the soil of Africa. It was January 12 1997. An overpowering feeling of *deja vu* came over me. Was it possible to relive something I'd never experienced before? At that moment, a strong urge to make a dramatic statement dared me. I was tempted to kneel and kiss the ground, just as the Pope does when he visits a new country. I resisted this ritual only because I didn't want the other four hundred passengers and crew thinking I was strange. After all, a Senior Banker with a major Canadian institution is supposed to behave conservatively, shouldn't she? I have to uphold the image. Being on vacation doesn't give me licence to behave outrageously, does it?

Those who have emigrated from their native countries can relate to what I felt. It's a feeling I get every time I return to my native country, Jamaica, and it doesn't matter how many years have elapsed since my last visit.

Feeling like a queen on her throne, I descend the steep aeroplane stairs. I look out toward the glorious land, sky, trees, houses and people. I expand my diaphragm full throttle allowing the country's fresh, oxygenated air to filter through my lungs. Slowly, step by step, I descend the bare metal stairs. I'm at the final rung; my feet touch the tarmac. Bingo! A certain feeling engulfs me, capturing my entire being. I belong here; this is my land ... nostalgia of years gone by, memories of joy, love, sadness, all rolled into one come racing toward me. This was the feeling that permeated my being when I touch Ghana's soil.

Africa, finally! My diaphragm contracts, air escapes and I hear my heart pounding in my chest. Forty six years after birth, I'd made it to the real homeland. Excitement bubbled up inside me. My emotions took off on a roller-coaster and now I stood at the top of the track—it was almost unbearable. The many frustrations and uncertainties I'd experienced before finally boarding the aeroplane in Toronto, were now behind me. What further difficulties could I encounter? I was in Ghana, the land of my forefathers. It didn't matter that I knew no one there, or that I had no hotel reservations. Flying thousands of miles from Toronto to Amsterdam and then to Accra was a feat in itself. The time had come to explore and enjoy Ghana. Later, I would move on to Nigeria. Time to descend that steep roller-coaster track ....

As I walked across the tarmac with a group of the first passengers to disembark the aeroplane, a gust of wind welcomed us. The gentle, warm kiss of Africa caressed my face like the kiss a mother plants on the cheeks of her new baby. I breathed in deeply and felt intoxicated. I wanted to laugh out loud, to do a hop-skip-and-jump. Instead I retrieved the little disposable camera from my tote bag and took a picture of the jumbo jet. Recently I'd been travelling with disposable cameras after having little success with the more expensive ones. Cheap cameras have never let me down. It seems I was truly intoxicated when deplaning for when the films were printed on my return home to Toronto, the picture of the jumbo jet was the only lopsided one of the bunch. At that moment, as I moved toward the main airport building, I saw the sun slide slowly downward in the western skies. It was 7:50 p.m.

Waiting anxiously in the immigration queue to be processed, I observed the man at the head of the line. He'd allowed two other passengers to proceed before him. He was now immediately in front of me.

"Are you not going forward?" I asked him politely.

Curiosity overrode any shyness I had. Who in their right mind wants to hang around an airport after a seven-hour flight? Certainly not me.

"I'm waiting for someone," he replied.

I assumed he was waiting on a particular immigration officer. His voice was pleasant, and he seemed respectable enough, so I decided to chat with him. Although excited about being in Ghana, I began to feel a little nervous. The reality of the moment hit me like a slap across the face. I was a single woman alone, who had travelled practically across the globe to a country I knew little about and where I knew no one. Although my cousin, Peabody, had given me the name and telephone number of one contact, I'd never met the person before, and no arrangement was made for him to meet me at the airport.

"Are you Ghanaian?" I asked him.

"Yes, I'm from here." Oh great, I thought, let me see if he can help. "Your accent, you're not Ghanaian?" he seemed curious about me now.

"No, I'm Jamaican-Canadian. I'm visiting your country for the first time. Maybe you can suggest a good hotel where I can stay?"

I didn't have hotel reservations because my travel agent, Mohammed, informed me he couldn't make arrangements for me from Canada.

"Sure, I'll help you, just wait for me after you collect your luggage," he offered without hesitation. Shortly after, I watched him stride toward an elderly officer at the far end of the room.

When my turn came to be interviewed by an immigration officer, I proceeded beyond the red line to the counter. The interview went smoothly for I had a visa and all the required documents for my entry to Ghana. I moved on toward the luggage carousel. I waited for what seemed like forever. Why is it every other passenger seems to have a suitcase that looks exactly like yours when you're searching for your own? As I moved my head looking from one end of the carousel to the other, I felt as if I was watching a tennis game. "The darn suitcase better show up soon or I'll get a crick in my neck." The hundreds of passengers waiting to collect their luggage dwindled to a few dozen.

When I looked around several minutes later, there were only six passengers remaining. I mused aloud if I could be so unlucky. What if my luggage was sent to France or Morocco or some such place? What a predicament to be in ... no luggage, no hotel reservation, and alone in a strange country thousands of miles from home! Finally, I spotted the suitcase on the conveyer belt. I dashed over and grabbed it before it went around again.

With luggage in hand and all cleared by Customs, I was ready to leave the airport.

"Oh there you are! What took you so long? I've been waiting

outside for you," my new-found acquaintance said. He'd returned to the baggage area to look for me.

"I'm sorry. I think my luggage was the last to come off the plane," I said, grinning at him.

He took the suitcase from me, and we walked toward the exit.

"I will take you out front. While you were inside, I arranged a taxi." When he saw the concerned look on my face he added, "The drivers here are pretty good."

Outside, we stood at the curb of the waiting area. He lifted his hand and beckoned to someone in the brightly lit parking lot. A small Peugeot stopped a short distance from where we stood. I was perturbed at the sight of the battered looking car. The paint was peeled; there were dents and scratches all over. It was difficult to determine whether the colour was white, cream or tan. I was about to ask the stranger if I could get a newer model when a six-foot-six figure unfurled himself from the car. I looked up mesmerized at the sight of the figure moving toward us. He had a body like Michael Jordan, tall, slim, athletic, with broad shoulders, and narrow hips. But something captured my attention—his face, he could have been the twin brother of one of my favourite actors—Wesley Snipes. Lean face, high cheek bones, flaring nostrils, and thick, dark, moist lips. His black hair was cropped so low, I could see his scalp glistening in the twilight. He wore a loose fitting cotton shirt, opened at the neck, and a pair of beige slacks. On his huge feet, they must have been at least size fourteen, he wore a pair of brown perforated leather shoes and no socks. He caught me staring at him and grinned, exposing a perfect set of teeth that were as white as newly fallen snow. As he caught me in a deadlock stare, I looked away, toward the stranger at my side.

While the tall man put my suitcase in the trunk of his car, locking the doors, one by one, my new friend assured me that this driver was the best. He owned his taxi, was a trained mechanic, was safe, trustworthy, and knew the city of Accra very well.

I thanked the stranger for his kindness. In a flash, he was gone. I never learned his name, nor did I see him again, but it seemed, whoever, or whatever he was, he set a "help Yvonne" syndrome in motion that I can only describe as mystic. How else can I explain the overwhelming kindness and helpfulness I experienced from total strangers during the rest of my stay in Africa?

As I sat in the back seat of the taxi, waiting for it to merge into the stream of airport traffic, I clutched my purse and tote bag tightly in my lap. I noticed that although the driver locked the car doors, he kept two of the windows opened, the driver's side and the back right windows. Fear gripped me. Suppose a pair of hands came through the back window and grabbed my purse? I would be totally traumatized. Images of me running around with no money, no passport and no phone numbers, sent my heartbeat into a tailspin. It wasn't that I was being paranoid; this is a Third World country, and one hears many stories about thieves in these places. The same scary feeling consumes me when I visit my native Jamaica. When I'm out in the streets, I don't wear any real gold or expensive jewellery and I clutch my purse under my arm as if I'm attached to it. Why should Ghana be any different? The driver must have sensed my discomfort or maybe he was watching me in the rear-view mirror, because he turned his head and looked back at me.

"Yuh don't have to worry about robbery here, yuh are safe."

Mmmmm, what a voice!—deep, sensuous, and comforting. I loved the sound of it. The voice of James Earl Jones was about one octave lower. He was right, too. With his reassurance, I never worried about robbery after that day. I always felt safe wherever I travelled in Ghana. Maybe having this man at my side most of the time contributed to that safe feeling, but I'm not sure that was the reason.

"So what's your name?" I asked. We had joined in the stream of traffic leaving the airport grounds.

"My name is Adamson Money."

At first, I thought he was joking. To my knowledge, Adamson is a surname, and surely no one has a last name of Money, especially an African? Didn't they always have weird names like Mabuta and Kakulatombo? Who was this guy trying to kid?

"So what is your name really?" I asked again, this time more demanding.

"It is Adamson Money, I spell it M-o-n-e," he replied with a note of confidence and authority. Ooh, I like a man who is sure of himself; wimps I can't stand. I think this Adamson and I will get along just fine. I felt I could trust him already, just as the stranger had inferred.

"My name is Yvonne Blackwood," I said. "Please take me to a nice hotel that is close to downtown and not too expensive."

The first hotel Adamson took me to, stood in semi-darkness, with no one at the reception desk. After we waited a few minutes, a man sauntered over to ask if he could help us. The hotel didn't appear to be hungry for business, and I didn't get a warm fuzzy about it.

"I'd prefer another hotel, a bit more upscale," I said to Adamson. "Why did you take me to that hotel?" I asked after we were travelling along the main road.

"Sorry, Miss, I wasn't sure what type of hotel yuh wanted. I tink I know now."

Moments later we arrived at the Paloma Hotel. It met my specifications. An attendant opened the gate when we arrived and directed us to a designated parking area close to a courtyard. Built like a kind of compound, Paloma's buildings are arranged in a square, surrounded by a low wall. As you enter the gate, to the right is an outdoor gift shop which sells carvings, drums, and masks. Beside it is a small bookshop with magazines and second hand novels. Looking through the books the next day, I discovered that no African books are included; they are all Euro-centric. Beyond the bookshop stands a unique restaurant. Elevated above a courtyard, you enter it by ascending four steps. The right side, surrounded by a low wall, overlooks the nearby street. While dining, you can watch the traffic. The restaurant's wooden roof is covered with dried palm leaves which gives it an African hut look. It seats about fifty people. To the immediate left are the kitchen and takeout counter. Further left are several boutiques including a liquor store.

Later in the week, I was disappointed when I tried to purchase Ghanaian booze at the liquor store and discovered they sold only South African liquor. Not that I have anything against South Africa, far from it. It was great to get South African products in Ghana, without having to travel all the way to that country. It truly delighted me. It all seemed so long ago now, but in the early nineteen eighties, I contributed my small bit toward South Africa gaining its freedom by attending Arts Against Apartheid functions, participating in candle light vigils, and praying for that country in Toronto. No one was happier than I, when Nelson Mandela was set free. Now, however, I wanted liquor made in Ghana. As they say, "When in Rome ... "

The central part of the square houses a gleaming, white three-storey building adorned with a bas-relief. The bas-relief carved in bronze, depicts an African celebration. This building contains the suites. A small bandstand with a thatched roof similar to that of the restaurant, stands in the middle of the complex. The rest of the area consists of a well-manicured lawn, a small children's playground, a ten-car parking lot and a cobbled courtyard. Instead of sitting in the covered restaurant, one can sit in the courtyard under the stars to dine or have a drink and enjoy the band. Later, I observe that a steady stream of patrons visits the restaurant or come for the entertainment which is open to non-guests of the hotel.

I enter the hotel suites by ascending a flight of stairs, while Adamson trudges behind with my suitcase. We pass through a narrow hallway which doubles as a sitting room. It has two comfortable couches, some chairs and a television set. Straight ahead is the reception desk. Provided someone is sitting at the desk, no one can enter the building without being seen. This provides some comfort. Interesting carvings are displayed in this area and African watercolour paintings adorn the walls. All are available for sale.

The young man at the desk is businesslike and friendly.

"Hello Miss, can I help you?" He flashes a bright smile as we enter.

"May I have a look at one of your single rooms?" I ask.

He removes a set of keys from the wall behind him. "Sure Miss, please come this way."

He leads me to room number nine on the same floor, and Adamson follows closely behind. The room is fresh, airy, and most important, clean. It contains all the amenities I need for a week's stay. A mahogany bed with a firm mattress, a colour TV, a well-stocked Mini Bar with bottled water, chocolate bars, pop and beer. A black telephone sits on the night table. I snatch it and listen—dial tone. Great! The small bathroom is antiseptically clean with a white tile shower stall, and white, cloth, shower curtains. I turn on the shiny chrome faucets and hot and cold water flows quickly. One definite requirement—the room must be air-conditioned; it is.

"I'll take it," I said once we return to the reception desk. The young man produces the required registration form and while completing it I ask, "What's your name?"

"Humphrey," he replies.

Adamson and Humphrey took my luggage to the room, then

Humphrey returned to his post at the front desk.

Humphrey became my good friend and protector for the rest of my stay at Paloma. He took particular care to phone me every morning before he finished his shift at 8:00 a.m., to check if I was all right and to take my order for room service breakfast. Humphrey wrote all my telephone messages on note pads, and instead of putting them in the guest's cubby hole at the reception desk, he slipped them under my door. I felt loved and special. I thought, where else in this world can you get such unsolicited care? He was a college student studying business administration, but worked nights at the hotel to help pay his tuition. Later in the week he mentioned that he wanted a pen-pal from Canada and asked me to help him find one. I promised to try. The other daytime staff, Yvonne and Gregory were also very helpful and friendly.

Standing in the centre of the room, I surveyed my home for the next week. The room was similar to an average hotel room in any country I'd visited. In fact it was much nicer than the Urbis hotel where I stayed in Paris a few years earlier. Why was I surprised? I snapped out of my thoughts when Adamson spoke.

"I will write my name and phone numba for yuh," he said.

"Use this," I said as I ripped out a page from the back of my diary and gave it to him. After writing, he handed me the paper and said, "I want to take yuh anywhere yuh want to go. Please call me if yuh need me. Don't use anyone else."

His last sentence was almost a command. He gave me his white-toothed grin, then added, "Welcome to Ghana Miss Yvonne, and have a good night."

"Thank you very much, Adamson. I'll call you tomorrow," I replied, accepting the paper with his phone number. My assessment of Adamson was to be proven correct. He was decisive, confident, but not overbearing.

The ability to assess people is a skill I've developed over the years during my banking career. Meeting people from all walks of life have honed that skill. It was Shakespeare who said that all the world's a stage and the men and women merely players. That is a lesson I've learned well. Quick study of a character can be crucial at times, and although I'm never 100 percent correct, most of the time, I am dead on in my assessments.

With two giant strides, Adamson left the room. Finally alone, I sat on the bed and pinched myself.

"Ghana, Land of my forefathers!" I said softly.

An exhilarating feeling cruised through me like the feeling a prospector experiences while digging for gold and finding hints of it. In this case, evidence confirms there is gold in the seam, but the unknown factor is, how much is there.

It was too early for bed, and I was too excited to sleep even if I wanted to. I was also disoriented by the time difference. Ghana is five hours ahead of Toronto, which meant my body clock thought it was early afternoon instead of 10:00 p.m.

After spending a leisurely half hour putting away my toiletries, hanging a few garments and freshening up, I locked the door behind me and walked with light steps toward the reception area.

Humphrey looked up and smiled. "You going out already Miss?"

"Yes, I'm going downstairs to see what's there,"

"If I can help with anything, please let me know."

"Thanks, Humphrey, I will."

I descended a dozen or so stairs, crossed the courtyard, and walked into the hut-look restaurant. It seemed like a busy spot for most of the tables were taken. A stout, middle-age white man sat alone at one table. I assumed he was a tourist and moved toward his table.

"Hello there, do you mind if I join you?" I asked as I flashed one of my charming smiles.

He looked me over from head to toe before he replied. I sensed he thought I was trying to pick him up. You should be so lucky, I thought.

"Feel free to sit," he replied.

"Thank you." I sat, then looked straight at him. "Are you a visitor here?" I asked.

"Yes I'm a visitor but I've been here a few times. I'm from Montana," he said with an American drawl.

"Oh really? I never figured you for an American."

"I thought you were African. Obviously from your accent you're not. By the way my name is Garry."

"I'm glad you thought I was African. I don't want to look like a tourist. I'm from Canada. Just arrived a couple of hours ago. I'm Yvonne."

I'd endured five long hours at my hairdresser in Toronto while he wove shoulder length braid extensions into my short black hair. With my dark skin and the braids, I'd hoped to blend in with the natives. It seemed to be working. We shook hands and Garry relaxed, then smiled at me.

"Can I buy you a beer?" he asked. He was already half way through the one he was drinking.

"Sure, thanks for offering. What do they have here?"

"I like the Star Beer. I'll get you one."

He ordered and while we waited for the waiter to bring it to our table, out of idle curiosity, I tried to find out a few things about him. Garry was evasive. I wasn't particularly interested in him, so I didn't attempt to probe further. After he finished his beer, he got up to leave. I thanked him again and we bade each other good night. I saw Garry once more during my stay at Paloma. He was with a gorgeous, black woman, so beautiful, even I had to take a second look. They were heading toward one of the suites, the floor above mine.

— ◇ —

The sun pelted down on me through the windshield of Adamson's car on the afternoon of my second day in Ghana. I was sitting in the front seat of the Peugeot (I never sat in the back seat again), while the vehicles moved slower than molasses in the Accra rush hour traffic. We were going to the crafts' market. I wound the window down to get more air and to gaze at the scene. Emerald flora covered the landscape, reminiscent of my homeland. In fact, it could have been any Caribbean Island, but I had assured myself by pinching my arm the night before, that I was in Africa. Luxuriant vegetation swayed in the breeze; many of the trees were covered in blossoms. Smiling black faces stared at us from every direction. Many looked familiar. They could have been brothers, sisters, aunts, uncles or cousins. The buildings, constructed from concrete blocks or wood, were similar to Caribbean architecture. This is home I thought as I took it all in.

A few minutes later, Adamson applied the brakes, jerking us forward. We were at an intersection, and the stoplight had changed to red. Within seconds, peddlers swarmed the car, selling cassette tapes, carvings, bottled water, all kinds of wares. Adamson shooed them away, speaking in dialect. I wanted to patronize one or two of them, but he warned me if I did, it would get worse, for more would swarm the car. Too bad I thought, but I took his advice. We travelled a little further in silence, then I turned and looked at him.

"Are you married Adamson?"

I asked the question, not because of any interest in him, but he seemed like too much of a nice guy to still be single. As they say, the good ones are always taken.

"I was married, but my wife died nine months ago. She was expecting a baby and de baby died too, dat is all."

Adamson habitually added "Dat is all," to most of his sentences, but when he said "all" it sounded like "oil." It added colour to the way he spoke. I was shocked at his answer. I wasn't prepared for it, and didn't know what to say.

"Oh ... Oh," I stuttered. "I'm so sorry. If you don't want to talk about it, please don't."

"I still can't believe she's gone," he continued as if in a trance. He snatched a photograph from the glove compartment and handed it to me.

"Dis was my wife. I love her very much," he said passionately. "We were married for less dan one year."

I scrutinized the photograph. The face of a very attractive, plump, young woman with a most disarming smile stared back.

"I'm really very sorry, Adamson," I said again softly as I returned the photo.

I didn't know what else to say. Losing one's spouse at such a young age was bad enough, he was in his early thirties, but losing your first child at the same time was a double whammy. He continued as if he didn't hear me. Suspended in time, he recounted the entire funeral event, detail by detail as if it occurred yesterday ... how he didn't cry; how he made all the arrangements; how he dressed his dead wife, and how he carried her body—alone. Tears welled up in my eyes, for I could see graphically what he was saying. I blinked them back; I couldn't let the tears escape, couldn't let him see how soft-hearted I was. From that moment I felt a kind of tenderness toward Adamson. I tried to understand him, to talk with him, to give him advice and encouragement. I knew that despite the constant bright smile on his face, he was hurting inside. Maybe his faith kept him going, for I soon learned that he was a devout Muslim, and he tried to pray five times each day. Whenever we were out on the road, and he missed a prayer moment, I always felt terrible. He would assure me it was all right, because he made up for it the next time he prayed. A special bond developed between us.

"Tell me something, Adamson, I've been meaning to ask you this. How do you get your teeth to be so white?"

I was burning to ask him that question from the moment he first smiled at me, the night before, when we met. It bothered me even more when I discovered later, that he smoked cigarettes. I saw him only once with a cigarette in his hand, for he never smoked in my presence, but I saw packets in his car. Knowing he is Muslim, I didn't think smoking was allowed, but what the heck, everyone has a vice.

"Is easy," Adamson replied. "My mama teach me. I use de chew-stick to clean dem fust, den I rub some charcoal on dem and clean dem, dat is all."

"That is all you do to keep them so white?" I rephrased the question.

The answer was unbelievable. I know no one who brushes their teeth more often than I do, and I use all the fandangled toothpastes for whiter teeth ... with baking soda, with peroxide, and goodness knows what else. I even bought a Chinese toothpaste called White Kiss and still my teeth didn't come anywhere close to Adamson's white teeth. And I don't smoke either.

"Yes, dat is all." He gave me a wide, white-toothed grin, so I could see for myself.

"Chew stick eh?" I repeated thoughtfully.

My mind floated back to the first time I'd seen chew stick. At the time, I thought it primitive. It was during one of the fun summers I used to spend in the hills of St. Andrew, Jamaica, with my paternal grandparents and several of my city cousins. A yearly ritual since I was eight years old, I spent most of my summer holidays with them. After my mother's death, when I was two years old, I grew up with her parents in Manchester, the south-central part of the island. It was therefore fitting that I spend some time with my father's relatives.

On one of these summer holiday visits, Bunny, one of my city cousins, introduced me to chew stick. It was a slender vine which grew wild in the bushes. The country folks chopped the vines down, then cut them into three inch lengths. One end was crushed to expose its fibres. Bunny showed me how to rub the crushed end over my teeth like a tooth brush. The chew stick produced a natural sud similar to toothpaste—not as tasty of course. I recalled using it a few times, but reverted to my toothbrush which seemed easier to use. I didn't know about the use of charcoal though. After hearing Adamson's explanation for white teeth, I surmised the use of chew stick was a tradition brought to Jamaica from Ghana.

An hour or so later, we eased out of the snail-paced traffic and entered the gates of the crafts' market. It's one every tourist to Ghana should visit. I went hog wild over stalls and stalls of carvings. There were large and tiny ones, drums, masks, walking sticks, wall plaques, busts, full figures. Anything that could be carved was on display. Many kinds of wood were used, mahogany, cedar and the indestructible black ebony. I purchased a few small pieces, but my main treasure was a waist-high mother and child carved from mahogany. Intricately detailed, the delicate folds of the mother's two-tiered dress, the head wrap, and the woman's jewellery were clearly depicted. The carving exuded passion, passion for the child that clung to its mother. It seemed the passion was quickly transferred to me where I became the mother and the carving the child. I wouldn't let the carving out of my sight when I had to travel. I took off and landed several times with the carving in my arms just as if it was a baby!

Once I selected the piece, Adamson began to haggle over the price. He and the vendor spoke in dialect so I had no idea what was being said. Back and forth, they argued as I looked from one to the other. At one time, it seemed they were quarrelling. Eventually, I paid fifteen thousand cedis less than the original asking price. I was happy.

Now fifteen thousand cedis sounds like a lot, but the value of the Ghanaian cedis was interesting. Before I started my shopping spree, Adamson took me to the Bureau of Exchange within the complex, where I converted some of my travellers cheques. It was a moment in time when I felt extremely wealthy. At seventeen hundred cedis to one USA dollar, I walked away with 680,000 cedis for US$400!

We moved on to explore the clothing section. It was one of the few times in my life that I felt confused. The outfits were fabulous, the array of colours bewildering—Joseph's coat of many colours was nothing compared to Ghana's materials. The patterns were incredible and the styles irresistible. I didn't know which one to buy but I knew one thing, I wouldn't return to Toronto without a Ghanaian outfit. It was only a matter of where and when. As vendors beckoned for all shoppers to patronize their stalls, I couldn't decide from whom to buy.

"Yuh don't have to buy a dress here. Yuh can buy material and make one." Adamson realizing my quandary, gave me a suggestion.

"That sounds good, but can it be made in time before I leave? You know I don't have a lot of time."

"No problem, de dressmakers here, sew quick."

I accepted Adamson's suggestion and opted not to buy a dress at the market that day.

We visited another section of the crafts market, where I watched a middle age man hand weave, or perhaps I should say hand and foot-weave, the Kente cloth. He sat before a dilapidated-looking wooden contraption, and while he held spools of thread between his big toes, he used his hands to move parts of the loom back and forth. I watched awe-struck as neat, smooth Kente cloth rolled off the contraption with some unusual patterns. Adamson explained that the Kente cloth is worn by the Ashanti tribe, mainly the rich ones, for the material is expensive. He told me that each pattern had a meaning. Naturally, when I returned to Toronto it was with strips of Kente cloth, hot off the press!

Adamson smiled at me gently when he asked me to meet his family. I became quite excited because wherever I've travelled, a close-up view of how the local people live has always fascinated me. It provides a true education which text books cannot. We travelled through the back streets of Accra, where houses weren't grand but rundown and dilapidated, where fences weren't strong and painted but broken down and rusty, where children roamed in tattered clothing and where mango and almond trees grew on every property. After a few miles, we arrived at our destination.

He proudly showed me a simple, narrow, one storey building with several doors leading in from the outside. Each adult had their own quarters and entered through their own door. Plain, glass louvre windows were covered with modest, white lace curtains. The kitchen was a detached building, situated at the far left corner of the yard. Separate kitchens were common for the poorer class in Ghana, similar to some of the homes in rural Jamaica.

I looked at the small, ramshackled kitchen, and instantly recalled one summer holiday that I spent with my paternal grandparents up in the hills of Mavis Bank. It was eighteen miles from Kingston, Jamaica's capital, situated in rough country. I've never forgotten "the saltless food" incident.

Five grandchildren were spending the summer with our grandparents. Judith and I were thirteen years old while Dimples was eleven, Faye, fourteen and Bunny, the only boy among us, was sixteen. They were brother and sisters while I was a cousin. On this unforgettable day, I was designated to cook dinner.

The kitchen, similar to Adamson's, was a separate building, a rather crude structure, with a dirt floor, one small window, a couple of rough wooden shelves and a wooden bench. Cooking was done on an elevated fireside built from stones and dirt against one wall about four feet above ground. A stove was nonexistent. Two parallel iron rods were embedded in the wall and firewood was placed beneath them, stacked at angles similar to the way cowboys made their fires. An iron pot would be placed on the iron bars above the fire.

To lift the jet-black pot which was covered with soot from direct flames and smoke from the fire, I had to grasp the two small handles on either side to place it over the fire. The pot weighed a ton even when it was empty. With flames leaping all around, it didn't take long for the contents of the pot to gurgle and splutter. I sat on the bench and waited for the food to cook. When I assumed it was ready, I tested the contents with a spoon. Satisfied that the food was cooked, I grabbed two kitchen towels from the shelf and held the small handles on either side of the pot. Slowly, I tried to remove it from the fire. It seems I hadn't grasped the tiny handles firmly enough, maybe the fireside was too high for a thirteen-year-old, or maybe it was the sheer weight of the boiling pot, but it came crashing down onto the dirt floor! I jumped a mile in the air to avoid being burnt by the scalding water and barely made it. After thanking my lucky stars that I escaped being burnt, realization dawned on me. What do I do now? Food was sprawled all over the dirt floor. Grandma, grandpa and my cousins were hungry, all waiting for the dinner I was supposed to cook. A dark shadow suddenly blocked the light from the doorway and Bunny was standing there, looking at me. He surveyed the situation then offered his advice.

"Just pick up the food, scrape off the dirt, rinse it off with some water and put it back in the pot," he said.

The confidence in his voice told me he'd done this before.

"You won't tell grandma?" I asked timidly.

"No, no, it's our little secret," Bunny said and he burst out laughing. I didn't think it was funny. As a matter of fact, I wanted to cry. I'd wanted so much to impress my grandparents because when the holidays were over and the day came for us to return to our homes, they always gave us gifts of money. I didn't want to do anything that would jeopardize my share of the loot.

Working quickly while Bunny stood guard, before anyone else decided to drop by the kitchen, I picked up, scraped and rinsed slices of breadfruit, pieces of yams and flat, round dumplings. I held the hot food with a kitchen towel and a fork, and any particles of dirt that my eagle eyes detected were quickly removed from the food. Bunny help me to put the pot back on the fire and I added more water. Soon the food was submerged and boiling merrily. Shortly after, I served freshly cooked food to my grandparents and my cousins.

As we sat at the dining table on the semi-covered verandah, I stole quick glances at everyone to see if they suspected anything but all seemed fine. Bunny and I exchanged fleeting glances and winks. Halfway through the meal, grandma said,

"Yvonne, the food is fresh, didn't you put any salt in the pot?"

Taken by surprise at grandma's question, I stuttered, "Yes ... yes ma'am. May ... maybe I didn't put enough."

By this time Bunny's wink had expanded to a grin. Then like the sun rising on a July morning, his grin was transformed into laughter. I looked at Bunny and wanted to kill him but all I could visualize were the contents of the boiling pot tumbling to the ground. It seemed to happen in slow motion.

I start laughing and now Bunny and I are laughing and we cannot stop. Grandma and grandpa are looking at both of us as if we had just landed from Mars. My other cousins are now coming alive with funny grins on their faces for they have no idea why we are laughing.

"Be quiet you two. What's so funny? Mind I don't give you something to laugh about," Grandpa yells.

I can see he is getting angry. If there is one thing old people detest, it is when you laugh and they don't know why. They're sensitive that way. Well, that makes us laugh even harder, and Judith, Faye and Dimples start laughing and soon they are cracking up too.

"Shhh!" Grandma signals with her pudgy shhh finger in front of her mouth that is filled with food. The sight of grandma shhh-ing us with her mouth full like that just pushes us over the edge and we all start howling, the kind of laughing that makes elementary school teachers send you outdoors to cool off. Then, all of a sudden, Grandpa stands up, all six feet two inches of him. He turns on his clunky boot heels and moves toward Bunny at the other end of the table. At this point, there is no stopping us. We couldn't stop laughing even if we wanted to. Looking at grandpa's funny, angry face just makes us scream with laughter. Grandpa had never spanked any of us but I'd never seen him so mad before. I knew it was all my fault and had to think quickly.

I sobered up. "Do you really, really want to know what is so funny Grandma and Grandpa?" I asked innocently, trying to save us all.

"Yes, we want to know," they replied in unison. Grandpa stops suddenly in mid stride and glares at me—waiting.

"Well, okay," I look straight at Bunny before he could open his mouth and say, "Bunny passed wind."

Well, the whole dinner table just rocked and rolled. My cousins started laughing and howling and Judith, Faye and Dimples all starts making pooping sounds with their mouths. I am laughing so hard I have stitches in my side and can hardly catch my breath.

"Get away from the dinner table this minute," Grandma commanded in her most serious voice.

Bunny knew he was in a jam and decided the only way to end the madness was to leave the table. I knew that I now owed him not one, but two.

Adamson's front yard was large, secured by a whitewashed stone wall. A huge mango tree grew close to the gate, and it was covered with blossoms, while green and ripe mangoes hung from the branches. It provided good shade for the otherwise bare front yard. He introduced everyone while we stood in the front yard. His sisters greeted me warmly, hugging me as if I was a part of the family.

There were two sisters, their four children, and his youngest brother. Adamson was anxious that I meet his parents, but they were away, praying at a nearby mosque when we arrived. He expected their return before my visit ended. A third sister lived in Kumasi, several hundred kilometres away, while his oldest brother had emigrated to Brussels, Belgium and a third brother lived in the United States. Adamson was the oldest son still living at home, and he explained how this placed a lot of responsibilities on his shoulders.

When he finished the introductions he said, "Dis is my home, dis is my family, dat is all."

As we sat on wooden benches in the yard, I talked with Adamson's sisters, who spoke some English, but not as fluently as Adamson. Although all the tribes in Ghana speak their own languages (his family was from the Hausa tribe) English is the medium of communication, therefore, I could speak with most of the people I met. While speaking with Adamson's sisters, I saw his younger brother and the children talking excitedly, huddled in one corner of the yard, giggling and chatting. Now and again they looked over at me then resumed their positions. I felt my ears become hot, and I knew they were talking about me. I asked Adamson what they were saying.

"Dey want to know if I'm going to marry you, dat is all," he looked at me, a big grin spreading across his face.

I almost choked. "Please assure them it is nothing like that," I offered quickly.

Marry Adamson! They must be crazy. Where on earth did they get that idea? We came from different worlds. There was no possibility that I could fit into his. It was also impossible for him to fit into my world for that matter. The culture, language, religion, social status, everything was completely different. I had no doubt he would make a native woman very happy, for he exhibited the qualities of a good husband, kind, considerate, hardworking, very attractive and a good listener, but definitely not for me. I put that ridiculous thought aside and concentrated on the surroundings.

At one point Adamson and his younger brother were embroiled in a heated exchange. Adamson appeared very serious and did most of the talking. The discussion was in dialect, so I couldn't understand what was being said. When the discussion ended, Adamson came and sat beside me.

"What was that all about?" I asked.

"I was telling my broda about someting he did dat was wrong. I have to show him de right way."

"But does he listen to you?" I asked. It seemed the young man had argued vehemently.

"Yeah, he listen, but he always have some excuse."

I smiled knowingly. Teenagers are the same wherever one travels.

They know everything.

— ◇ —

"Adamson, I would love to try your mangoes. Are there any ripe ones?" I had been hungering for the mangoes on the tree since I arrived and couldn't resist any longer, I was anxious to taste one. They looked similar to a type I knew in Jamaica, besides, I love mangoes.

"Yes, no problem. Boy, get de stick," he shouted to his brother.

In an instant Adamson's younger brother pointed a long stick with a hook at one end into the thick foliage, and two ripe mangoes crashed to the ground.

"I want to eat them now. Can you wash them for me?" I asked the brother. He washed the mangoes and gave them to me. I began to eat one of them. As if an alarm sounded, Adamson said, "I have to pray now. Can yuh excuse me?"

"Sure, go ahead. Just forget I'm here."

He walked solemnly to a corner of the yard beyond the mango tree where a large piece of cardboard lay on the ground, close to the fence. That must be the shrine I thought. I watched in awe as he carried out the prayer ritual, facing east, bowing head to the ground, rising and repeating his devotions.

While Adamson prayed in one corner, his two sisters excused themselves, covered their heads with shawls they wore around their shoulders, and they too began to pray in another corner. The praying involved kneeling and touching the ground with their foreheads. I had never seen anything like this before, except in the movies. As a Christian, I knew very little about the Muslim religion at that time. Suddenly, I stopped eating the mango. Gingerly, I held up the half-eaten fruit with its succulent peach coloured flesh exposed. Sweet sticky juice trickled slowly down my right wrist to my arm, then cascaded off my elbow to the ground. I was afraid to continue eating while Adamson and his sisters prayed, in case it was construed as a sacrilegious act. I waited and watched and was relieved and pleasantly surprised when the prayers ended in less than ten minutes. I finished the first mango, washed my hands and mouth, then put the other in my purse for another day.

The children needed to be fed, and I watched Adamson's older sister dish up bowls of fu-fu and bowls of soup. The children collected their meals and sat in the yard to eat. Usually fu-fu and soup are eaten together. Fu-fu is a dough-like dish made from boiled cassava and plantain pounded together in a mortar. It is a local staple food that Ghanaians eat regularly.

Adamson had introduced me to fu-fu the previous day. We were out touring the markets and other places of interest when he suggested we dine at a homely little restaurant. He assured me the food was good there. It was dinner time and I was famished. Being adventurous and a lover of exotic foods, when Adamson suggested we order fu-fu, I agreed to try it. I recalled my grandmother making something called fu-fu when I was a small child but I soon discovered this wasn't the same thing. Adamson instructed me how to eat it.

"Fust, yuh wash yuh hands. See the bowl?" He pointed to a bowl filled with water sitting on the table. I washed my hands and dried them with the paper towel provided. "Yuh use only yuh hands to eat it."

"What, no fork or spoon?" I asked, trying to figure out how it would work. Since being acquainted with cutlery from early childhood, I'm one of those people who, when given the opportunity, will eat pizza with a knife and fork.

"No fork, no spoon," he said firmly. "Now yuh cut it wid yuh finger, like dis." Adamson demonstrated with two fingers acting scissor-like. I followed his instructions awkwardly.

"Now yuh dip it in de soup and swallow it." Adamson put a piece of fu-fu in his mouth and swallowed. I did the same, or tried to do the same. I couldn't get the darn thing down my esophagus although I tried very hard. I opted to chew it. I chewed and chewed and chewed some more, right through the entire meal. It felt as if I were chewing bubble-gum. I couldn't finish it; my jaws were too tired. Adamson was upset. I got the feeling that it was important for me to like fu-fu.

"So you don't like my fu-fu?" he said accusingly.

"That's not true Adamson. It's quite tasty with the soup, but I just can't swallow it the way you do." I never tried it again.

I was disappointed that I never had an opportunity to meet Adamson's parents for they had not returned before my visit ended.

While the children ate, Adamson invited me to see his quarters. It didn't surprise me that everything was neat and tidy. From the first time we met, I noticed that Adamson took particular care with his appearance. His clothes were always clean, neat, coordinated, and he always smelled good. Typically automobile mechanics have black dirt under their finger nails but not Adamson, his were well kept and clean. I remember the day he wore a sky-blue, loose fitting African shirt with rich, white embroidery at the neckline, accentuated with a pair of white slacks and a matching pair of sky-blue snake-skin shoes!

In one corner of Adamson's living room, a soft blue light glowed, giving the room an aura of tranquillity. Two sets of chairs were arranged around the room. They were similar to ones commonly found in the Caribbean. Their polished wooden frames had low backs, and were upholstered in a navy blue cloth. A wooden coffee table with carvings engraved in it stood in the centre. A metal wall unit occupied one wall and a stereo set was neatly stacked inside. A picture of Adamson's wife graced the wall above the wall unit. It was a blown up version of the photograph he'd shown me in his car, the day we visited the crafts market.

A white cloth screen divided the room and I assumed his bedroom was behind it. We chatted for a while, and I sensed that he was nervous having me alone with him in the quiet quarters. My thoughts raced. I wondered what his family was thinking as they sat in the yard talking. Was some significance being placed on my visit? I couldn't help remembering what the children had asked. Were they reading more into the visit, more than I intended it to be? I looked at Adamson and I could see his eyes gleaming as he stared at my body, even in the pale blue light.

P A D D Y

hen I first arrived in Ghana I was determined to enjoy it to the fullest, to explore it, learn about it, eat, sleep and drink it. I intended to absorb every bit that I possibly could. It was a long way from home, and I knew I wouldn't return for several years. I hoped when I departed, to take a piece of it with me forever lodged in my heart.

My one preoccupation, however, was to secure a visa to Nigeria as soon as possible. Later, sitting in my hotel room before going to the restaurant for a drink, I'd picked up the telephone and dialled.

"Hello, Mr. Bishura? Paddy? My name is Yvonne Blackwood. I'm visiting from Toronto, Canada. My cousin Peabody Benjamin gave me your name and number, and suggested I call you."

"Oh, you're Sister Benjamin's cousin?"

"Yes, I just arrived in Accra."

"How is dear Sister Benjamin?"

"She is very well and sends her regards."

"Welcome to Ghana. I hope to see you soon, but I'm extremely busy on the job right now. Where are you staying?"

"I'm staying at the Paloma Hotel."

"Good, that's not far away. Give me your number, and I'll call you. Maybe we can have dinner one evening."

Have dinner one evening? Is that all he planned? I'd anticipated an excited Paddy, rushing over to collect me, offering me accommodation in his home, making plans to show me around, doing all the hospitable things I always enjoy doing for my visitors. What about sightseeing, dinners, visiting friends? It seemed this was not to be. Calm down, Yvonne, this is a different culture. I concluded that knowing I had one contact in the country was comforting, although I felt disappointed at his reaction. It wasn't that I needed help, somehow, I'd gotten the wrong idea of how I would be received from my dear cousin Peabody.

— ✧ —

Peabody lives in Rochester, New York, which is a three and a half hours drive from my home in Toronto. We visit each other several times a year. I remembered clearly the weekend I spent with her the previous October. We sat around the table in her spacious kitchen. From the wide window, I gazed at Peabody's large backyard garden which used to be a swimming pool. Fall flowers bloomed in profusion; clumps of orange and yellow chrysanthemums, pink delphiniums, and purple asters. Her two adult daughters had joined us and we were chitchatting as we always do, while we drank Peabody's wicked cucumber juice. We were having a wonderful time as we tried to out do each others stories.

Peabody told her stories in an amusing way. She would stand before us, switch to Jamaican dialect with all the inferences and gesticulations, and you couldn't help cracking up with laughter as you watched her. My son, said (not in her presence of course) she looks like an Ewak when she laughs. Kids can be cruel.

One of her famous lines was, "Yvonne Blackwood-Jacken, fe me house a fe yuh house, yuh a me fambly!"

Visiting them was always fun.

"Hey Peabody," I said, "I'm planning a trip to Africa. You know how much I've wanted to go there for sometime."

"Oh Yvonne, that will be wonderful. Which countries are you going to visit?"

"Ghana of course, and Nigeria."

We'd shared the same grandmother, and she'd heard the same grandma's stories that I knew. She'd spent the early part of her life growing up with Grandma Eliza and knew about our great- great-grandfather declaring that he was Ashanti. She could relate to why I chose Ghana.

"Let me give you the name and number of one of my church brothers. He lives in Accra. I think he's wealthy because when his wife became ill, he sent her here for treatment."

"Treatment? What kind of treatment?" I asked.

"The dear soul had cancer."

"Oh, that's terrible. What happened to her? Is she okay now?"

"You know only people with money can afford to get treatment in this country. I nursed her for a while when she came but poor thing, the cancer was too far gone; she died."

"I'm sorry to hear." I replied not knowing what else to say.

"You never know, Paddy may put you up when you get there," Peabody continued.

She rummaged through the small drawer under the telephone table, found Paddy's number and wrote it on a slip of paper. She handed me the paper and I carefully tucked it away in my purse.

Later that night, we'd all retired to bed when the telephone rang. I heard Peabody talking excitedly from her room at the other side of the house. Moments later she burst into the guest room.

"Yvonne, you will not believe this." She was flushed and agitated. "That was Paddy Bishura, my church brother, calling from Ghana. That phone number and address I gave you earlier? It's his!"

"You're right; I don't believe it. So, did you tell him about me? That I'll be visiting his country soon?" I could feel a tinge of excitement, all trace of sleep being suspended for the time being.

"Sure, I did. Do you know," Peabody continued, "I haven't heard from him in over a year, and out of the blue he calls tonight?"

Interesting coincidence, I thought, but soon the incident was forgotten.

— ◇ —

I surveyed my hotel room, and realized that I was truly on my own. I concluded that if Paddy couldn't take time out to see me, I'd forget about him. All my energies must now be focused on obtaining a visa for Nigeria, or I would spend my entire vacation in Ghana. I don't think I would have minded too much if I had to spend all of my time there. Everyone seemed friendly and loving. I felt at home, but I knew Joyce was waiting anxiously in Nigeria to hear from me. I couldn't let her down.

I called Adamson early next morning and he responded promptly. Immediately after breakfast, he arrived at my hotel and we set out for the Nigerian High Commissioner's Office. I was very confident I would get the visa with little effort. After all I'm a good citizen, I carried all required documents, and Mohammed, my travel agent, had told me it would be "no problem" to get a visa in Ghana.

We drove along Ring Road where several attractive high-rise office buildings stood. Many looked similar to some of the office towers in Toronto. Roads were clogged with rush-hour traffic but Adamson burrowed through it like an earth worm in wet soil, as he negotiated every opening he could find. Before long we arrived at the High Commissioner's office. Adamson argued with the guard at the gatehouse who wouldn't allow us to drive in. Eventually, he opened the high metal gate and instructed Adamson to park in a far corner.

I waited an hour before being ushered into a large room with several desks and as many people. A large, framed picture of General Sani Abacha, Nigeria's president, hung prominently on one wall. He was dressed in full military regalia, and seemed to be looking directly at anyone who entered the room. The Passport Officer, a slim black man, offered me a chair at his cluttered desk. I retrieved my passport and letter of invitation from my handbag and explained to him that I needed a visitor's visa to Nigeria. He looked over the documents with little interest, then with a smug look on his face, he smiled as if he knew something I didn't.

"I can't give you a visa from here," he said.

"What do you mean, I can't get a visa from here?"

I tried hard to remain calm as I spoke to him. I knew one thing you never do in these countries; never allow government officials to get mad at you. They can be very vindictive and can make life miserable for you.

"You should have gotten the visa from your own country," the officer spoke slowly as if addressing a person who didn't understand English.

"But I couldn't. You no longer have an embassy in Canada, and I couldn't get through to your New York office." I lied because I'd tried, but with no success.

I pleaded in my most imploring voice. "Look Officer, my sister-in-law is waiting in Nigeria for me. I can't afford to come this far across the globe without seeing her. What can I do? There must be an exception you can make for a visitor?"

The officer looked at me with a smirk on his face. I wanted to kick him under the desk. His eyes told me he had no pity for me.

"Sorry Miss, you have to tell your sister-in-law to apply for a visa for you in Nigeria. She can forward a copy to us here, then you can go."

He dismissed me like a naughty child. I was devastated.

I rejoined Adamson in the reception area. When he saw the look on my face, he asked what was the matter. I gave him the disappointing news. Adamson tried to console me, suggesting we drive across the border to Nigeria to get the visa there. That may have worked but I hated to do things on a whim. Besides, I had no idea how many hours it would take to travel to Lagos or what other problems it could entail. I pulled out the little map of Africa from my diary, and checked it over. There were two small countries between Ghana and Nigeria, Togo and Benin. We could get stuck in one of those countries for all I knew. I also didn't want to spend days out of the short time I had travelling unknown roads. I told Adamson, "Thanks, but no thanks."

Earlier when I tried to contact Joyce, I'd learned that it was just as difficult to contact Nigeria by telephone from within Africa as it is from outside. Besides, it would have taken much more than one week for Joyce to obtain a visa and mail it to Accra. I had to do something. I wouldn't allow anything to deter me from visiting Nigeria. I remained resolute that my plans would work out. I had faith.

— ◇ —

Adamson drove me to the hotel where I relaxed for a while.

With no one to turn to, I swallowed my pride and called Paddy at his office.

"Paddy, I'm sorry to impose on you, but I'd planned to spend two weeks of my vacation in Nigeria, and I tried to get a visa this morning but they turned me down. Can you help me in any way?"

"Where are you now?"

"At my hotel."

"Don't leave your hotel. I'll send my driver over in an hour. Have your passport ready. The driver will take you to see a friend of mine who I think can help you." He rang off.

Within an hour, Paddy's driver arrived in a late model, shiny, dark-blue BMW. I was impressed. It confirmed Peabody's idea that Paddy was wealthy, for BMWs aren't cheap cars by any stretch of the imagination. Louis the driver, was a small man of about thirty. He had a pair of lazy eyes. I was never quite sure when he was looking at me. Louis spoke very softly, and smiled a lot. He called me Sister Yvonne. I think he assumed I belonged to the same church denomination as Paddy. I didn't dispute it. He informed me that we were going to visit a Mr. Quainoo.

Mr. Quainoo lived in a huge house surrounded by a high fence. When we arrived, an attendant opened the gate and allowed us to enter. The two-story building was landscaped with tufts of shrubs and a huge mango tree at the front. Louis and I climbed a steep flight of stairs where we met another servant who ushered us into a large sitting room. A glance at my watch, showed it was noon, but the house was as quiet as a tomb. The heavy drapes which were drawn across the windows casted an aura of semi-darkness over the room. Somehow, the atmosphere evoked the need to whisper and walk on tiptoe.

After a few minutes Mr. Quainoo swaggered into the room. Dressed, in a wrapper, a traditional African garment worn inside the house, he looked terribly dishevelled. Despite the loose wrapper draped over his body, I could see a large pot belly protruding beneath. He had two red, bulging eyes and a large black mole on the right side of his nose. He was not a handsome man. In fact, he was ugly. When he greeted us with outstretched hands, his piercing, high-pitched voice surprised me. He proved to be one of the most pleasant persons I've ever met.

"You must excuse my appearance," he apologized. "I don't normally take visitors at this time. It is our religious holiday period. I have been fasting for many days. I'm very weak." He spoke in short jerky sentences, as if he was running out of breath.

"I'm the one who should apologize Mr. Quainoo, I had no idea about the holiday. What is it?"

"Ramadan," he replied.

I felt silly and uninformed. I'd heard about Ramadan, but I didn't think it was that time of the year, nor did I know that Mr. Quainoo was a Muslim. Like the layers of an onion, my ignorance of Ghana was being exfoliated day by day leaving me exposed and naked. Later I learned that almost two-thirds of Ghana's population are Christians while the major part of the remainder is Muslim.

Mr. Quainoo consoled me, telling me not to worry about disturbing him, and we discussed the situation with the visa. I waited anxiously to hear the subject of money mentioned, but it didn't surface. Mr. Quainoo told me to leave my passport with him and I would be contacted the next day.

I hesitated as my mind shifted into overdrive. What? Leave my passport? With a total stranger? What if he sells it or duplicates it? I had heard enough about forgery in the banking world to know that this could be a dangerous thing. Besides, Canadian passports seemed to be a favourite for such activities in these parts of the world. But what else can I do if I'm to get the visa? In any event, he was Paddy's friend.

Paddy wouldn't put me in touch with unscrupulous people, would he? But I haven't even met Paddy yet, maybe he is a crook! But my cousin Peabody wouldn't put me in touch with a crook. Oh, but this man is religious; look at him, he is even starving himself for the sake of religion! And most important, he didn't ask me for any money. I decided I must trust someone, and it seemed Mr. Quainoo had the ability to help me. I returned to my hotel minus my passport.

On the way back, Louis took me to Paddy's house which was only a few minutes away. It was a large sprawling, one story house with a garden in front. A profusion of colourful dahlias and gladioli populated the garden. A silver Mercedes Benz was parked in the carport. Yes indeed, thought I, this Paddy fellow ain't starving for sure, a "Bimmy" and now a Mercedes. No starvation here! Inside, the house was spacious and tastefully decorated. I concluded that Paddy's wife must have been very sophisticated.

Louis called Paddy on a cellular phone, then handed it to me. While we spoke, Louis busied himself in the kitchen, preparing refreshments. It seemed Louis was not only Paddy's driver, he was also the odd-job man.

"Hello Yvonne, please make yourself at home. How did it go with Quainoo?"

"Thanks, Paddy. I think it went well. He said he'll call me tomorrow. I hope it will be with good news."

"I'm sure it will be. Quainoo is an influential man. Sorry I can't see you today, but soon."

"I understand. Thanks for all your help, and I'm looking forward to meeting you." He hung up. I was no longer upset with Paddy; a man has to do what a man has to do.

After I had the refreshments Louis served: thirst quenching, freshly squeezed orange juice, and an assortment of crackers and cheese, he whisked me back to my hotel.

Next morning, the shrill ringing of the telephone woke me from a restful sleep. Mr. Quainoo's high pitched voice slithered through the line, "Hallo Yvonne, I want you to go back to the Nigerian High Commission's office at noon. Ask for Sam, the same fellow you saw yesterday."

"Is he going to give me the visa now?" I asked, my voice filled with doubt.

"Don't worry about it. Sam is expecting you. Just make sure you ask to see him. By the way, take two passport-size photos with you."

I thanked Mr. Quainoo and he rang off.

Adamson arrived at my hotel an hour before noon and on the way we stopped at a small photo studio where I took some instant passport pictures. At the High Commissioner's office, we waited together in a closed waiting room, anxious for my turn to come to be interviewed. We were the only ones in the room until three men dressed in flowing, colourful robes entered.

A constant chatter in dialect followed between them. I was intrigued by one of them in particular. He must have been seven feet tall, thin, with the tiniest face imaginable. He reminded me of men on stilts in the Caribana parade in Toronto. He wore a light blue and white robe and carried a purple and white kettle. Now why would someone be travelling around with a kettle, I wondered. I was itching to take a picture of him. Eventually, I walked over to the skinny man.

"Can I take a picture of you?" I asked as I retrieved my camera from by purse. The man stared at me as if I was a strange creature. The shortest man in the group spoke.

"He don't speak English, Miss." His accent was as thick as chunky soup.

"I hope you don't mind, I'm a tourist, and I would like to take pictures of all of you. Is it okay?" He nodded his head, giving me a shiny gold-teeth grin.

"What do you fellows do?" I asked while trying to line them up for the shot.

"We cowboys," the spokesman said.

My imagination went galloping on that one. Cowboys eh? I couldn't quite see them rounding up cattle in those robes and sandals. Not like the cowboys of the Wild West with their tight pants and boots with spurs. Maybe they were shepherds? That would be a little less athletic. I conceded—to each his own.

"What's the kettle for?" I asked.

Adamson, sensing I was asking too many questions, chipped in, "Dey're Muslims. Dey carry water in it. Dey must touch water five times a day."

I took a couple photographs, and thanked them kindly. They left the room shortly after. It left me wondering if the flash bulb had scared them off. I hoped they didn't think the camera had taken away their souls or anything of that nature!

Nearly an hour elapsed while Adamson and I waited. We began to gasp for breath. The closed room was windowless, and the air-conditioning unit, stuck in one corner, produced more noise than cool air. The musty room smelled like mildew. I could almost hear the molds growing! Unable to stand it any longer, Adamson opened the door, and we rushed out of there as if our clothes were on fire. We stood in the lobby the remainder of the time until the receptionist informed me that it was my turn.

Adamson stayed behind after wishing me good luck. I entered the office not knowing what to expect. There was a noticeable difference from my first visit. Sam, the officer who had turned me down the previous day, no longer smirked at me. Today, he seemed pleasant and tried to make small talk. He even smiled. I handed him the US$30 he requested and in return he gave me a receipt for US$20. I didn't question the discrepancy for I left the office with a Nigerian visa stamped in my passport. I should mention that at that time, ten US dollars converted to seventeen thousand cedis, enough to buy lunch for a week. Whatever transpired between my first visit and the second, I have no knowledge, and I asked no questions. I only knew I was as happy as a pig in mud. I was going to Nigeria after all!

I never spoke to or heard from Mr. Quainoo again, and I was never asked to pay any money. Back at my hotel, I thanked God for sending Mr. Quainoo to help me. After my big panic attack that I would never make it to Nigeria, it had all worked out so easily. I relayed my thanks to him through Paddy.

Paddy helped me in other ways during my stay in his country but during those days we never met. He volunteered his driver to take me around, and it would have been exciting to cruise around town in his shiny air-conditioned BMW, but I used his services only twice. I tried not to upset Adamson, who made it his duty to show up at my hotel each day whether I called him or not.

On one occasion when I used Paddy's driver, Louis took me to a dressmaker to have a dress made from a piece of material I'd purchased at one of the roadside markets. The material was a colourful tie-dyed cotton with earthy tones. Olive-green, yellow and mustard colours all ran into each other as if an artist had splashed a paint brush with a mixture of all these tones across it. The blend of colours made me feel warm and alive. Having had a difficult time deciding which dresses to buy the day I went shopping with Adamson at the crafts market, I decided to take him up on his suggestion, and purchased material that I liked so that I could have a dress made to my specifications.

Pearl, the dressmaker was an attractive woman about twenty-two years old. She lived in a small room behind a store. The room was just large enough to hold a double bed, a chair and Pearl's foot-pedalled sewing machine. The rusty zinc roof had no inner ceiling which would have helped to absorb the direct sunlight. Pearl fascinated me. She took my measurements nonchalantly, only jotting down a couple things. I was sure she wouldn't be able to make a dress to fit properly based on the sketchy information she had written down. I gave her a quick description of what I wanted her to design and left.

Three days later Louis took me to collect the outfit. Pearl left the small room to chat with him while I tried on the dress. When she returned five minutes later, I was drenched with perspiration. Sweat poured down my face and back. The room felt like an oven. The slight exertion to remove my clothes and to put the dress on, coupled with the closed door, had magnified the Ghanaian heat ten fold. I wondered how Pearl could possibly work in that furnace.

My question was answered when I looked in the small mirror she held up for me to view her handiwork. It was stunning. I looked like a regal, African princess. I couldn't wait to get back to Toronto to show it off. Pearl had designed a three-piece ensemble consisting of an ankle-length skirt with a provocative slit up one side; a jacket with rows of neat tucks and six exquisite buttons that looked like "sprinkles" on a cake; large puffy sleeves; and a head piece. If I had given her a pattern to use, the outfit couldn't have been made better. The sewing was neat, and the job was perfect. When I left that hot sticky room, my thoughts were, what a wonderful businesswoman Pearl would be if only given an opportunity.

— ✧ —

My face-to-face meeting with Paddy was my first and only. It took place on my last day in Ghana. Louis arrived at my hotel at noon and we loaded up my suitcase, overnight bag, and carvings into the BMW. His mission was to take me to have lunch with Paddy, then for a quick tour around Accra, of areas I hadn't seen, and finally to take me to the airport to catch a 5:30 p.m. flight to Lagos.

Paddy was waiting for me at an upscale Chinese restaurant on the second floor of a two-story building. Louis escorted me to the table and Paddy rose to greet me. He wrapped his strong arms around me, kissing me on the cheek and I felt as if we'd known each other for years. He pulled out my chair and I thought, Wow! chivalry is alive and well in Ghana. He smiled at me as we chatted, and we sized each other up. He was a medium-built, good-looking man in his mid fifties. He had a slight paunch, and specks of grey dispersed throughout his hair. He looked very aristocratic dressed in a light blue suit and a blue shirt with contrasting white collar. I was dressed casually in blue jeans and a colourful purple, green, and yellow Hawaiian shirt, with white running shoes. I'd tied my braids back with a purple scrunchie. Soon, we were talking like old friends.

One of Paddy's associate joined us for lunch, and he promptly introduced me to Dr. Tom Obeng, also an attractive man. He didn't say much during the meal, but Paddy made no secret that had he known I was so attractive he would have found some time to meet me before. He ordered several Chinese dishes, and I wondered how three people could possibly consume all that food. Paddy's choice from the menu was impeccable. The meal was sumptuous. Tom and I struggled to compete, but we were no-match for Paddy. That man could eat!

"Paddy, I want you to know that I'm eternally grateful to you for all your help." We were sipping our liqueurs lazily at the end of the meal. "Do you realize that although we're meeting for the first time today, without you I probably would not be going on to Nigeria?"

"My dear Yvonne," he said, as he touched my hand on the table, "it was my pleasure to do the little that I did. Too bad you are leaving. Things have slowed down on the job, and I now have more time. Such a pity." He seemed genuinely sorry.

"I had some kind of premonition, if you can call it that, that you would play an important role during this trip."

"How's that?" Paddy asked, looking at me with raised brows.

"Do you recall one night last October when you called my cousin in Rochester?"

"Yes I remember, she told me about you at the time."

"Well, you called her in less than an hour after she told me about you and gave me your number. She said it was more than a year, she hadn't heard from you. I thought it odd that you called at that precise moment. I've always wondered how you'd fit into the picture."

Paddy gave a hearty laugh and squeezed my hand.

S I G H T S   O F   G H A N A

"I have sown the seed and indeed it will germinate."
~ Osagyefo Dr. Kwame Nkrumah

*T*hat quotation, printed on the small entry ticket to the Kwame Nkrumah Park, was certainly thought provoking. An exuberant Adamson wanted to show me the attractions of his country and I, the excited, born-again-found-my-roots visitor, was anxious to see them, to see everything! Who could want a better tour guide? He was handsome, witty, and knowledgable. A list of places of interest to visit, a standard item that I always secured whenever I travelled, was nonexistent because I knew so little about the country. I'd heard about Cape Coast, however, and that was one place I wanted to see. But time was limited. The difficulty I experienced in obtaining a visa for Nigeria, robbed me of valuable time. I therefore left it up to Adamson to chart our course of exploration.

One of the first landmarks Adamson took me to see was the Kwame Nkrumah Memorial Park which housed Nkrumah's mausoleum and monument. On a hot sunny day, a couple of hours before the sun reached its ultimate intensity, we arrived at the park. Adamson drove slowly, almost reverently up the long driveway, allowing me time to take it all in. When we eventually reached the parking lot, it was empty. It indicated that we would have the place to ourselves, at least for a while, and that suited me fine.

The park occupied a large plot of land with well-kept gardens, pruned green trees and exotic flowers. Red and yellow butterflies darted from one pollen-filled flower to another, and little birds chirped from among the trees. It was a park where a visit shouldn't be rushed. I wanted to move slowly through it, savouring, caressing everything with my eyes. Just beyond the park, a stately red roof building nestling among the trees, peeked through at us. Adamson said it was the old parliament building.

The mausoleum was an imposing, futuristic-looking structure, hewn from what appeared to be variegated, grey granite. A larger-than-life statue of Nkrumah, stood on a large pedestal in front. He was dressed in a flowing African robe, with his left fist clinched, and his right hand pointed ahead, as if to say, "let's go forward, people." Inlaid in the centre of the pedestal, an engraved bronze plaque read:

"Dr. Kwame Nkrumah 1909-1972"

Immediately in front of the monument was a dual fountain separated by a paved walkway. Inside each fountain, two rows of statues depicting atetenben players, crouched on pedestals. The players appeared to blow into the hornlike instruments and out spewed crystal clear water, while thin arches of water cascaded over the entire fountain.

"I don't know if yuh know about Nkrumah?" Adamson asked. History came flooding back. "Yes, I remember hearing about him when I was in high school in the nineteen sixties."

"He was our fust Prime Minister after we got Independence from British Colonial Rule in 1957." Adamson sounded as if he rehearsed that reply, but it explained a lot.

"If I remember correctly, he was well known and well respected all over the world," I reflected.

"Yes, he was famous; he really helped all of Africa and de people loved him."

It was apt that Ghanaians honoured this great man.

The statues were expertly crafted and very lifelike. Inspecting them closely, I concluded that Ghanaians must be amongst the most gifted craftsmen on the planet. As the days went by, I was convinced of it, for every carving, every statue I saw, and I saw many, was of very artistic quality.

"This is lovely, Adamson," I said, while I taking in a panoramic view of the park. I wanted him to know I appreciated his first choice of places to visit. Adamson flashed me his white-tooth grin, confirming that he was pleased.

"You should see dis place at night when dey put on de flood lights."

Unfortunately, time would not permit a night visit, but I could imagine the fabulous rainbow effect the lights would have on the cascading fountain.

Nkrumah's tomb occupied a special place inside the mausoleum and was cordoned off by a rope barrier. I scrutinized a large framed painting of Nkrumah which was placed on the tomb. He was dressed in a colourful Kente robe, and he looked young, handsome and regal. Several of his personal paraphernalia were displayed inside the mausoleum, and numerous photographs taken with many heads of state lined the mausoleum's walls.

I was checking out the tomb when I realized there were no other visitors around. The lone guard, I'd seen earlier, must have gone for some fresh air for I couldn't see him anywhere. It was just Adamson, the Tomb, and me. Mischievous thoughts played around in my head. Should I or shouldn't I? In one smooth motion, I sneaked over the rope barrier, climbed on top of the tomb, and posed. Can you believe it? I posed on top of Nkrumah's tomb! Then I asked Adamson to take a picture—quickly. Always willing to oblige, he did just that. For one nanosecond, I felt as if I had lived a tiny bit of history. From that moment on, I became more pumped up to enjoy the sights and sounds of Ghana.

A long stretch of white sand beach, turquoise water, clear blue skies with fluffy white clouds floating about, red and yellow bamboo beach umbrellas anchored in the sand, an outdoor semi-covered bar encircled by thick-foliage trees, a tropical sun pelting down on my face and arms; this is Labadi Beach. Without forewarning, Adamson had taken me to Ghana's famous beach. Labadi Beach Hotel, built right on the beach a short distance from the ocean, is Accra's only five star hotel. I would have loved to stay there, but I couldn't afford it, at least, not for any length of time, but the beach was open to the public. On this day except for the gateman, two staff, and a couple of tourists (probably guests from the hotel), there was no one else on the beach. Since I hadn't planned a beach outing, I had no bathing suit with me. But the ocean looked too inviting not to feel its wetness on my skin. I rolled up the legs of my jeans, and kicked off my running shoes and socks. Adamson looked at me admiringly, then followed suit. Together we strolled along the fine, white sand beach.

— ✧ —

For a brief moment, I was transported somewhere else. I couldn't imagine this was Africa. Isn't that odd? I never associated a beach with Africa. When I thought of Africa, I thought of land mass, forests, towns, villages, and farms. Of course, I also thought of the stereotypical starved, half-naked black people, with bulging eyes and taut skins stretched across their ribs as depicted by the media, but I never thought of a beach. The bathing suit tucked away in my suitcase was there from force of habit, a standard vacation item, and not because of any plans to bathe in Africa's ocean.

Looking across the vast expanse of water, I conjured up a map of Africa. I could see West Africa. I put an imaginary finger on the spot. Yes, there it is. This marvellous, shimmering, turquoise body of water is the Atlantic ocean. It could easily have been Doctor's Cave Beach in Montego Bay, or Grand Anse Beach in Grenada. I gazed steadfastly at the Atlantic and realized it was the same ocean I'd bathed in at Cocoa Beach, while visiting Florida a couple years earlier! Come to think of it, the Caribbean Sea which surrounds my homeland Jamaica, and all the other Caribbean Islands, is really an extension of this same ocean, the Atlantic. Yes, whoever said the world is a small place, is right.

Barefooted, Adamson and I strolled along the warm sand, tempting it to caress the soles of our feet. Occasionally we allowed white frothy water created by receding waves to splash over our feet. His loose fitting, white cotton shirt billowed in the wind while my shiny braids whipped across my face. I felt as if the salty air was cleansing me, taking away all life's experiences and troubles, leaving me young and innocent, with all thoughts of life in Canada erased. I stooped to cup my hands full of water and splashed it over my face. Smacking my lips, I tasted the salty Atlantic ocean.

Except for the lapping of the waves, everything was calm and serene. We were both absorbed in our own worlds, when suddenly, like a pebble tossed into a motionless pond creating giant ripples, the air was shattered by a loud noise from the sky. I looked up to see a small plane performing dangerous manoeuvres.

"Oh my God! Someone is attempting to commit suicide," I yelled above the roar of the motor. The small plane plunged from the sky at a hundred and eighty-degree angle toward the ocean. I held my breath, waiting for the impact and explosion. I didn't want to watch it crash but curiosity kept my eyes glued to the plane. Just before it hit the water, it soared with a roar up, up, into the sky again.

"Hey, I bet dat is J. J. Rawlings." Adamson looked up at the plane admiringly.

"J. J. Rawlings? I know that name," I said, trying to make the connection. Lately, my memory hasn't been as sharp as it once was. I don't worry about it as much as I used to, after some of my girlfriends mentioned they were experiencing a similar thing. Information overload, I call it. Just too many things to think about, the job, a thousand forms to remember, hundreds of products to know, dozens of tasks to perform, personal life with household chores to take care of, bills to pay, and always another function to attend. Is it any wonder that the mental machinery needs overhauling occasionally? A friend created an acronym for it, C-R-A-F-T. She had us in stitches when she told us the meaning— "Can't remember a flipping thing!"

"Sure, you know. He is our President," Adamson said.

"Get out!"

"Get out of what?" Adamson asked, looking inquiringly at me.

"Oh, I don't mean getting out of anything. It's just an expression." When I saw the wide-eyed innocence of Adamson's face, I gave up. "Never mind. You mean to say, that is the President of Ghana flying that plane, doing those crazy things?"

"Yeah, he was a pilot before. Dey says when he get mad or bored, he jump in a plane and just fly!"

Although unbelievable, I was fascinated with the story. Adamson was adamant it was true, so I gave him the benefit of the doubt. We watched the plane manoeuvre a few more times, and then, as quickly as it had appeared, it vanished into thin air. If this J. J. Rawlings is as far out as Adamson makes him out to be, I'd love to meet him, maybe on my next trip.

Adamson broke my trend of thought. "Yvonne, we better head back home. We can come back here on Sunday when dey will have entertainment and lots of people."

"Sure, I'd love to return here to see the action."

— ✧ —

On Sunday afternoon Adamson and I returned to Labadi Beach. I did a double take when we entered the gate. The empty stretch of beach I'd seen on Thursday, was covered almost every inch, with people: black people, white people, brown people, all lying on colourful beach towels, beach chairs, or just spread out on the sand. Children built sand castles; others buried themselves in the sand; vendors moved between bathers carrying glass cases on their heads from which they sold snacks, while bartenders dashed back and forth serving drinks. Several more beach umbrellas were added to the ones I'd seen on my first visit. Some made from cloth, advertised Star beer and Heinekin.

Suddenly, drums sounded. I looked up from the umbrella table which Adamson had secured for us that we shared with three of his friends. We were drinking Star beer while Adamson sipped orange juice. As I sat in the intense heat I began to feel mellow, ready to soak up the entertainment. Close to the semi-covered bar was a slightly raised platform. A six-piece band consisting of drummers, and players of a few peculiar percussion instruments, had taken their seats quietly on stage. Drums sounded again and this time eight dancers, dressed in colourful costumes, pranced on stage. They began to dance to the beat of the drums. The dance steps were choreographed to depict different stories. Energetic dancers performed as if they had no vertebrae, supple bodies gyrating to the African rhythm. The audience stamped their feet and clapped their hands to the beat. It was contagious, I found myself doing the same. There is nothing quite like the beating of African drums. The sound resonates inside your chest, your heart, your very soul.

I closed my eyes. I felt that the drums were talking to me, calling me, welcoming me. I visualized my ancestors as if I were watching a three-dimensional movie, proud Ashantis, dressed in yellow, red and green kente clothing, strings of beads swinging around their necks and ankles, dancing, and laughing, free as wild mustangs. What a pure, happy life they must have enjoyed on the soil of this huge continent until ... I didn't want to think about the until. Yet vivid scenes from the movie *Roots*, flashed through my mind.

I saw young Kunta Kinte fresh from manhood training, being captured by some white men. As if he was a wild animal, they put chains around his neck, hands and feet. The frightened boy screams a blood curdling scream, a cry of desperation, hopelessness, of fear. No one comes to his rescue. Why, oh why, did this terrible thing happen to my ancestors? Before my tear glands began to spew, I forced myself to slip out of that reverie and return to the scene in front of me.

As I watched the dancers perform I deciphered one story easily: Two men competed shamelessly for the affection of the same woman. Soon the first suitor seemed confident he had won her heart and prepared to leave with her. The second man did not give up, instead he put on a spectacular display of passion and strength. The fickle young woman could not resist him and eventually said good bye to the first suitor and left with the second. The piece ended with the couple dancing a passionate dance of love and joy. One couldn't help feeling warm and tingly when their dance ended. The crowd applauded wildly after each performance.

After a short break, the dancers reappeared in grass skirts. The drum-beat became louder and louder, the dancers moved faster and faster. The crowd went wild. Two bathing-suit-clad members of the audience, a man and a woman, decided to put on their own show. They leaped from their seats and began to dance among the crowd. Competition was fierce between them as hands and legs flailed, and bodies gyrated never missing a beat. Laughter erupted; the crowd could not contain itself. The dance ended with thunderous applause. I wasn't sure if the applause was for the professional dancers on stage or the impromptu dance couple.

Shortly before the entertainment ended, Adamson stood up.

"Yvonne, I have to leave yuh for a short while. Can yuh wait here until I get back?"

"Sure, but where are you going?" I asked.

"I have to do some business wid my friends and dey want me to look at someting. It won't take long."

"Go ahead, but it will be dark soon. I don't want to be on the beach too late." It was dusk, and several people began to leave the beach.

"I'll leave my friend Sammy to keep yuh company. Soon be back, okay?"

I watched him and his two friends talking excitedly in *Ga*, as they left the beach. Forty-five minutes later, Adamson hadn't returned. After an hour, Sammy volunteered to go to the gate to look for him as only a few of the beach lovers remained. I sat alone at my table for a while longer, then decided I had enough. I was very annoyed with Adamson. How could he take me to the beach and leave to transact business? How could he leave me stranded at the beach at night, knowing that everyone would be gone by a certain time. This wasn't like Adamson at all. I headed toward the gate where I found Sammy still looking for his friend.

Although I felt safe in Ghana, I was concerned that I would have to stand at the side of the road to thumb for a taxi. Why tempt faith by allowing strangers to pick me up on the street at night? I recanted when I saw several taxis lined up outside the gate, waiting. Drivers competed ferociously for passengers, calling and jostling when people walked by. I took one driven by a sixty-five-year-old man. I figured he would be safe and waved goodbye to Sammy as we drove away. I hoped for his sake that he got home safely.

Back at the hotel, I headed straight for the restaurant, too livid to sit alone in my room. A stimulant of some kind was needed to return me to a sense of calm, to simmer me down. It had been a fabulous evening—hot African sun seeped into my every pore, the camaraderie of the people, exciting entertainment mixed in with nostalgia of what my ancestors must have enjoyed. All had culminated like a steaming bowl of pepperpot soup, blended to a creamy texture. Now the moment was lost, buried in my anger. Adamson had spilt the soup all over the darn kitchen floor! I wanted to rip his face off.

While sitting at a table in the courtyard under the stars sipping rum and coke, I had a clear view of the hotel's gate. I looked around to see if I recognized any on the patrons—not a one. The incident rested heavily on my mind. What was Adamson up to? What was so urgent that it couldn't wait for the next day. What was he thinking when he left me at the beach? He'd better have a good explanation and he'd better show up here to apologize!

I saw him the moment he entered the gate. No one could mistake his surefooted strides and arms as long as Yonge Street, dangling at his side. I pretended not to see him and looked in the opposite direction. Within seconds his tall shadow fell across my table.

"Yvonne, please, please forgive me," Adamson pleaded. "I never wanted to leave yuh alone, I was only going for fifteen minutes. I ..."

He tried to continue but I cut him off, "How could you do such a thing? How could you leave me, a stranger, alone on the beach at night?" I spat the words at him and they sliced through the still night air, sharp as a shard of broken glass.

"Please don't be cross wid me. I was so upset when I couldn't come back soon. Please believe me. I told my friends I have to go but dey wouldn't let me leave." He pulled up his chair closer to mine and held my hand. Electric sparks surged up my arm; I yanked it away. "Yvonne, I'm sorry from the bottom of my heart. Please forgive me. I will never do anything like dat again."

I loved the way he calls my name. I looked at his lean face, the thick dark lips. An African Adonis with clear pleading eyes, eyes that extolled innocence stared into my soul, and I melted. I felt a strong urge to hug him close, to brush my throbbing lips against his! Maybe he was right, maybe he didn't plan for this to happen and at least, he was man enough to apologize.

"Okay Adamson, I forgive you. Let's forget the whole incident ever happened."

Later, after he departed, I felt as if we had a lover's quarrel. I marvelled at how close we'd become in a few days.

Ghana was truly a welcoming country. The warmth I felt was next to none. I became so absorbed in it, I had no time to think of anything else. The evenings that I remained at the hotel, I spent talking and watching TV in the reception area with Humphrey and other local people. Listening and talking with the local people is an education no books can impart. I kept up-to-date with world news, the little I wanted to hear, by watching CNN International, one of many TV channels available.

One night, I saw a commercial on TV which put the whole race and slavery issue in perspective for me. It told me that Africa and in particular Ghana, had come a very long way from Colonial Rule. The commercial was advertising a Nashu fax machine. It went like this:

A white man sits in his office typing a letter on his typewriter, at some eighty words per minute. A black man stands at the desk watching him keenly. The white man, with a superior condescending attitude, tries to explain to the black man what he is doing. He concludes that he must now mail the letter. Assuming he has taught the black man a valuable, lesson, the white man beams proudly. The black man looks at him and politely asks, "Why don't you fax it?" The white man looks shocked. "Fax? What is that?" The black man takes him into his office and humbly shows the white man how to use a fax machine.

That commercial spoke volumes.

The day Adamson and I visited the crafts market, he also took me to downtown Accra to see another of their great attractions, Makola Market. Ghana has a population of fourteen million people, and one and a half million live in Accra. That day, it seemed that one million of them were at this market. I exaggerate, but really, many thousands were there. They lined the streets for miles. Adamson insisted that I remain in the car instead of walking amongst the stalls. For my sightseeing tour of the market, he drove, I'm not sure if it could be called driving, but he managed somehow to move the car along the streets, through the crowd. Everything imaginable was sold at Makola Market, from fruits and vegetables to livestock, clothing and utensils. Here pedestrians were kings. They took over the streets. Blaring horns did not faze them. Every vendor competed to be the first to sell their products to the passers-by.

Several women carried babies tucked in the small of their backs, partially covered with materials from the mother's clothing, something I'd never seen before. Where I grew up, babies are carried in one's arms or held up against one's shoulders at the front. In Canada, it is the same or the child is pushed around in a pram. It was fascinating to see angelic faces peering inquiringly from behind, wrapped securely among their mother's colourful clothing.

"Hey Adamson, look at the baby on the mother's back. How come they carry the baby like that?" I asked when I saw the first one. Adamson explained that every child should be carried that way.

"Why is that?" I asked, showing my ignorance of his culture.

"If de mother does not carry de baby in de back, he give a lot of problems, dat is all."

"Were you carried that way?"

"Yes, my mada carried all her children dat way."

I accepted his rationale. Who am I to judge? I supposed he meant some kind of bonding took place between the mother and child.

— ◇ —

I awoke refreshed and well rested to the ringing of the telephone. It was Humphrey with my regular morning call. I told him I wouldn't order my usual room service breakfast that morning, instead I would dine in the restaurant. After a shower, I dressed and skipped energetically down the stairs, and along the paved narrow pathway between the children's playground and the bandstand. Suddenly, I saw something move from the corner of my eye. I stopped dead in my tracks. A lizard with a cobalt blue head, scampered across my path. I couldn't move, I stood frozen to the spot.

When my mother-in-law complained to me about how she feared for her daughter Joyce living down in Africa, because she was deadly afraid of lizards, I hadn't volunteered a certain piece of information— I, too, am afraid of them. I don't relish the thought of those creatures being near me. As a child, I tolerated them for there were many tree lizards in the rural part of Jamaica where I grew up, but they stayed away from me and I from them.

When I was eleven or twelve, I had an incident that to this day, when I think about it, my hair stands on end. While playing alone in the yard, I saw a mid-size green lizard on an orange tree and decided to kill it. I retrieved a long stick from the yard and took careful aim at the sucker. With all the force I could muster, I brought the stick down on the lizard, laying so close to the orange branch it seemed attached to it. What happened next put the fear of God in me, and made me even more afraid of lizards for the rest of my life. In one split second after I brought the stick down on the lizard, I felt a cold clammy creature on my chest. The lizard, anticipating my deathblow, had jumped to save its life. It jumped on me! I ran toward the house screaming at the top of my lungs. I ripped off my scanty sleeveless top, exposing my secret budding new breasts. With all pride and modesty forgotten, I ran crying for help. In the meantime, the lizard, probably more frightened than I, ran along the ground. From a leaf-green colour, it had turned dark green, almost black, in an attempt to camouflage itself. Weeks later, I would awaken at nights, soaked in a cold sweat after vivid dreams that a huge, black lizard was chasing me. During the days, sometimes eerie feelings came over me as I felt the cold clammy sensation of the reptile on my chest. It took me a long time to forget the incident.

I relived that moment when I saw the blue-headed reptile scurrying across my path. After what seemed like several minutes, when I felt confident the lizard was gone, I continued the short walk to the hut-look restaurant. By the time the waiter placed my breakfast on the table, I'd lost my appetite.

This was not the only hair raising lizard incident I experienced in Ghana. Another day, sitting quietly at a corner table, I was having lunch alone at the same restaurant. My seat commanded a good view of all the patrons. There were a few couples, a group of blue-collar working men, a well-dressed black woman with an Indian couple, and two business men dressed in immaculate navy-blue suits and white shirts. I didn't envy their positions at that moment, for the temperature must have been, at least, 95 degrees Fahrenheit.

A young waiter dressed in a short-sleeve white shirt and black pants had just served the two business men and headed toward my table. He was in the middle of the room when two lizards darted out of his path and crawled under my table. My hair stood on end and my heart pounded like a Congo drum. I quickly pulled my legs up off the ground until my knees touched the table top. I forgot about pride and modesty and all the other ladylike things a woman does or shouldn't do. As luck would have it, I was wearing a skirt and blouse that day! Only when I was assured by the waiter that the lizards had been driven out, did I put my feet back on the ground. Lunch had little taste that day. I spent most of my time watching the floor for the creepy crawlers.

Wednesday night Adamson took me out on the town after we'd dined at my hotel. I was dressed in cherry-red narrow-legged slacks with matching V-neck top, while Adamson wore white slacks and a baby-blue shirt. Looking more handsome than ever, his Hugo Boss cologne tantalized me. He took me to see the Prime Minister's residence and some large homes including those of some of the diplomats residing in Accra. The area reminded me of Rockcliffe Park in Ottawa. The houses were fabulous. It was pleasing to see such beautiful homes in Ghana. Yes, just as I thought, there were wealthy black Africans, living more luxuriously than we can imagine, and they do it with such dignity.

Next, we went club hopping. We stopped at #1 Club. This was mainly an outdoor affair. Several patrons sat around tables anchored on a gravelled courtyard. A waiter steered us into the midst of the crowd to an umbrella table which had no umbrella. The evening was cool, the coolest I'd felt since my arrival in Ghana. Looking up at the sky, it was a blanket of blue, deep and mysterious. Stars glistened and shimmered above our heads while we listened to high-life music. Adamson ordered drinks, ABC Beer for me and non-alcoholic malt for himself. Adamson, always fun to be with, had a collection of funny anecdotes to relate while we relaxed.

After a while, we moved on to another club—Club Kilimanjaro. This was a modern North-American-style nightclub. Inside were small, low, round tables with comfortable leather upholstered couches. The lights were low, but on the dance floor, disco lights lit up the room as they flashed intermittently. The music was definitely American and mainly from the seventies era.

Momentarily, I'm transported back to Kingston, Jamaica, to the early nineteen seventies. I'm out on the town with Bernard, my ex, and Ivor and his girl Natalie. We drop in at Club Epiphany in uptown, Kingston. The night sounds are distinct: dogs barking in the distance, traffic passing by, the laughter of young people our age group, making jokes and taking jabs in return. My sense of smell is mercilessly abused by a thick odour from mixtures of perfumes, after shave lotions, hair pomade, alcohol and cigarettes. The smells hang heavily over the room. The Deejay put another 45 RPM record on the turntable. The first strains of the melody come softly through the speakers which are distributed throughout the room. I hear waves splashing. Bernard and I exchange loving glances; it's one of our favourites. Otis Redding belts it out:

"Sittin' in the morning sun,
I'll be Sittin' when the evening comes ...
I'm Sittin' on the dock of the bay ... "

It's incredible how this place, Club Kilimanjaro, thousands of miles away from my homeland, evoke such powerful nostalgia from the sanctum of my mind.

I looked across the small table, at the man sitting on the soft leather couch next to me. He's taller, (much taller) slimmer, his accent is different, his voice is more sensuous. I'm in Ghana, not Jamaica, and I'm with Adamson not Bernard. Dock of the Bay began to play. I couldn't resist; I asked Adamson to dance. We danced to several tunes.

He was no John Travolta, but he managed to keep the beat until the tunes ended. I could tell that my kind of dancing was not something Adamson did often. It was a fun night, and we hung out until early next morning.

On the way to my hotel, we stopped at a roadside street vendor. Adamson bought hot fried plantain, wrapped in newspaper, and small packages of groundnuts. (There peanut, is called groundnut.)

"Here Yvonne, try this."

Adamson handed me a package of the plantain and one of the nuts. I looked at him skeptically when I saw the newspaper. Is this guy for real? Does he expect me to eat food out of dirty newspaper?

"Tr..try it?" I stuttered.

When I made no attempt to open the packages, he said,

"Let me show yuh how to eat it."

He opened up the newspaper exposing the soft yellow-brown, fried strips of plantain. Then he removed a twist-tie from the saran wrap which contained the peanuts. He spread out both on the seat of the car. "Fust, yuh get some plantain." He picked up two or three pieces. "Den yuh get a few grains of groundnut," he rolled his "r" when he said ground, "den yuh put them in yuh mouth and eat it, dat is all."

He demonstrated by eating a mouthful of the stuff. I could see he enjoyed it. When I realized there was a wax-paper-lining inside the newspaper, I relaxed and agreed to try our late-night treat. I was accustomed to fried plantain, for it is a traditional Jamaican side-dish. The combination with peanuts was new to me, however, I ate a mouthful, then another and another, it was very palatable.

While we sat in the car on the street of Ghana, my mind wandered to my first visit to Barbados. One night my friend and host, Ron Blackman, had taken me to Baxter's Road where we bought food from roadside vendors. On that occasion we bought fried Flying Fish and a sweetbread of some sort, called leadpipe. As the name suggests, it was mission impossible to eat the leadpipe which was as tough as a concrete brick. My salivary glands worked overtime until it was softened enough to chew. There is a certain wild fun about eating food from street vendors. You do it with confidence that the food is clean and good. You do it for old time's sake. I experienced a similar feeling as Adamson and I sat in his car and ate fried plantain and peanuts. Once I got over the hurdle of the newspaper wrapping, there was no fear or concern. After we finished eating, he took me home to my hotel. It was deja vu; I felt like a teenager who had been out on a first date.

— ✧ —

One of Ghana's major tourist attraction is Cape Coast Castles. Slaves who were captured by Arabs, white men, or their own people and sold to the white man, were held in the dungeons of the castles at Cape Coast. The castles were used as holding pens until the slaves were shipped to North America and the West Indies. Some of the paraphernalia used to torture and apply inhuman punishment on the slaves, are displayed there. I've heard first hand from people who have visited Cape Coast, how horrible it is and how sad and depressing the trip made them feel. Some even broke down and cried, the agony of their ancestors being so vivid. When I left Toronto, Cape Coast was high on my agenda. But as the days went by and I began to enjoy Ghana and its people, to see its richness and its beauty, I fell in love with the country. I made a big decision. I wanted to remember Ghana as the happy, vibrant place I'd seen. I would not clutter the memory with anything sad and unpleasant. I decided not to visit Cape Coast … not this time.

*B*reathless with excitement, I fired questions at Adamson faster than he could respond.

"When can we go to Kumasi? Is it far? Is it a nice place to visit? Will I see some real gold?"

"I can take yuh dere on Friday."

Adamson grinned as he watched the excitement building inside me. Somehow he could read my body language and understand my moods. Although no academic, he was an intelligent, perceptive man. We were having lunch at my hotel's restaurant and through the open side, we watched the traffic whizzing by on the busy street a few yards away. On the radio, the last strains of "Take a bow," Madonna's duet with Baby Face, faded slowly. The music stopped to let the announcer make a few comments. Then, the unmistakable voice of Bob Marley filtered through the sound system.

"One love, one heart,

Let's get together and feel all right ... "

How profound, that that particular song should play at that moment. Sitting beside Adamson, enveloped in his Hugo Boss cologne, I felt like one of the people as Bob Marley belted out "One love." It was one of my favourite songs and one I grew up with. Over the years it has become his signature song, and deejays love to play it at the end of Black Community dances.

For a brief moment, I visualized a semi-dark hall with chairs stashed in corners, tables covered with empty glasses and bottles, pushed back against the wall to make more room on the dance floor. I can feel heat radiating from hot, sweaty bodies. Everyone is on their feet, swaying to the Reggae beat and mouthing the words of the tune. The deejay readjusts his headphone. Then, as the crowd is totally enraptured in the song, he stops the record. The crowd continues to sing "one love, one heart ... ," oblivious to the interruption. The deejay stops and starts the record intermittently all during the song while the audience continues singing, never missing a beat. Everyone has taken a stroll down memory lane. The dance ends with the party-goers on a high.

Listening to Bob Marley, I thought, Wow! My countryman is certainly international; he's known even here in Ghana. My wandering mind lazily returned to Adamson who sat smiling from across the table.

"So, how far is it?" I asked again.

"It will take us about five hours to drive dere."

The waiter appears at our table with a bowl of boiled yams and a steaming dish of something brown. I looked at the second bowl. No, it's not quite brown, all I could think of was guacamole and dark chocolate blended together. The pungent aroma wafting from the dish, hit my nostrils like a bullet. I'd ordered boiled yams with chicken and balava sauce, but I had no idea what balava was. I figured I would still have a belly full of yams if I didn't find it palatable.

After living in Canada for almost a half of my life, I'd slowly deviated from some of my Jamaican traditions including foods I once enjoyed as a youngster. But the heritage remains deeply rooted in my soul, fermenting, waiting to spring forward when the call comes. This was the call. Yams and sweet potatoes were staple foods during my childhood. Many days those tubers constituted 90 percent of the five food groups in each meal.

My grandparents with whom I lived, were farmers, and they cultivated almost everything we consumed. Coffee beans were sold to the coffee board and the unsold portion was parched and grounded to make Grandma and Grandpa's early morning "tea." Children were not allowed to drink coffee; the older folks always said it would stunt their growth. Our tea was brewed from all kinds of leaves—orange, peppermint, fevers grass—if it was a leaf, tea could be brewed from it! My grandparents cultivated acres of yams and sweet potatoes, which were sold by the hundredweight to higglers. When harvested only the best were sold. Many times we were left with tons of small yams and potatoes. After feeding some to the pigs, sometimes we didn't know what to do with the leftovers. My cousins and I would roast, boil, and bake these tubers. Sometimes we pelted each other with them!

As I eyeballed the plate in the waiter's hand, I thought, yes, I would have no difficulty filling my stomach with delicious yams. Adamson had ordered his favourite—fufu and chicken soup. His face lit up like an incandescent bulb when the waiter brought his meal. He certainly had a love affair with fufu. While he washed his hands in preparation for the fufu-eating procedure, I dug right into my meal. I wasn't disappointed; the balava tasted a lot better than it looked. Adamson explained that it was green leaves from a type of yam cooked up into a thick, dark sauce.

The immortal words of my great-great-grandfather, "I am Ashanti," formed the catalyst for the discussion I was having with Adamson. On my first outing with him, I told him a few things about myself, mentioning that my great-great-grandfather used to say he was an Ashanti.

"So yuh is Ashanti woman!" Adamson teased. "De Ashantis are de richest, most powerful tribes in Ghana. Most of our gold is on dere land."

From that moment, he took great pleasure in referring to the Ashantis as my people whenever we discussed them. He said each person, male or female, has a special name depending on the day of the week they were born. He wanted to bestow an Ashanti name on me but although I've been told the day of the week I was born, for the life of me, I couldn't remember it. I had to pass up on my Ashanti name.

"Did yuh know Ghana was called de Gold Coast before we got independence?" Without waiting for an answer he continued, "Yuh must visit Kumasi. It is de capital of de Ashanti Region."

I was elated! This would be a bonus. I never thought I would come this close to my roots. When I arrived in Ghana my initial plan was to explore Accra, for I'd never heard of Kumasi.

"You will see real gold at de palace," Adamson continued, as he answered my third question.

"Palace? They have a palace?" This was beginning to sound more exciting than I could imagine.

"Yes, a big one." Adamson seemed puzzled at my reaction.

"Do you know anyone there?"

"Yes, remember I told yuh, one of my sisters live dere?"

"Yeah, yeah, I forgot. Maybe we can drop in to see her."

"If dat's okay wid yuh. I don't want to use up yuh time." Adamson, always the thoughtful, considerate man, I was blessed to have him at my service. Sometimes I think about him and the strange way we met. My belief in destiny makes me aware that some people come into our lives to touch us because it is so ordained. Sometimes they collide with us for special reasons, to teach us a lesson or to guide us on a path, we never really know why. I kept asking myself, why did I meet this particular young man?

"You won't be using up my time, Adamson; it will be my pleasure to visit your sister." I didn't want him to feel bad about anything.

"All right, we will visit Mary," he said, offering his usual wide grin.

The decision to visit Kumasi was made for Friday. That night, I phoned Paddy to tell him about my plan. Although I hadn't met Paddy in person at this point, I felt it was important for him to know of my whereabouts. He seemed pleased to hear about the trip.

"One of my colleagues, Abu, lives out there. Let me give you his number. Please look him up and say hello."

He gave me both Abu's business and home telephone numbers.

I was ready for the adventure, and pleased to have at least one contact in Kumasi.

Adamson arrived at my hotel early Friday morning for the journey. I packed an overnight bag along with bottled water. I travelled everywhere in Ghana with bottled water on the advice from my doctor in Toronto. I also packed two boxes of tissue for my runny nose because I'd contracted a cold the day before.

The trip took us through a cross section of Ghana. Joyce's advice that this time of the year was the dry season, had me expecting to see parched shrubbery and dried grass everywhere—not so. Either the weather pattern had changed or the dry season was over, for verdant vegetation dotted the landscape. Beautiful undulating hills, thick with green plants and flowers greeted us.

I recognized several plants from the Caribbean. Many homes grew bougainvillaeas and they were in full bloom with beautiful red, pink, orange and fuchsia flowers. Almond trees were laden with fruits, their thick, shiny leaves gleaming in the sun. Several species of palm trees flanked the sides of the road, while I could see others like sentinels on the farm lands stretching for miles into the distance. Vendors sold reddish palm nuts in little piles at the sides of the road. They also sold red palm oil in plastic bottles which had been extracted from the nuts. I wasn't familiar with that particular specie of palm, and Adamson filled me in on its uses. Every aspect of the palm can be used for various things, but the most important thing was the palm wine. This was a specialty and very important to the Ashanti Kings. The wine apparently has the same mystique to Ashanti men as raw oysters have to Caribbean men. Need I say more! Patches of Cassava plants grew everywhere. The ubiquitous mango trees were covered with fruits and blossoms at the same time. Cocoa trees and banana trees were weighed down with their fruits awaiting to be harvested.

We drove along paved roads with many potholes. Most of the natural forest had disappeared, but occasionally snippets of the original came into view. On one of these occasions, we passed a thick patch of forest consisting of hundreds of tall trees that were almost branchless. Each could have been thirty feet tall with tiny, leafy branches jutting out close to their tops. Adamson said those trees were used specifically for electric poles. I could see why; they were ideal. We overtook a few trucks as they laboured slowly up steep inclines. In the open backs were huge timber logs that filled the rear platform of each truck. Timber is a big industry in some parts of Ghana, and Adamson explained that they were cut from the interior forest.

We came upon a few police checkpoints manned by uniformed soldiers with guns. At these posts, soldiers pulled over motorists randomly and questioned them. They seemed harmless however, and we had no problems with them. At one of these checkpoints, I witnessed the driver of a mini bus(a type of line taxi in Ghana) hand some cash to a soldier. The soldier, without as much as a side glance, took the money and promptly waved the mini bus through. I was appalled at the nerve of the soldier accepting what I assumed was a bribe so openly in broad daylight for all to see, and wearing his government's uniform to boot! Of course, I'd heard about corruption in Africa, so it was not a surprise, just the open way in which it was done surprised me.

"Adamson, did you see that?" I asked, condemnation heavy in my voice.

"Yes, I see him. Some of dese guys take bribes, but if J. J. Rawlings ever found out, dey would be out of a job tomorrow." From all accounts, it seemed J. J. Rawlings, the President, was well respected by most Ghanaians.

"How would the President know about it?" I was leery about Adamson's statement and showed it. Sometimes I wondered if he made up some of the stories for my benefit.

"You don't know dat guy. He know everyting! Dey say sometimes he drive around in a unmarked car, to see what de people are doing."

"Really, Adamson, he finds time to do that?" I said with a hint of sarcasm in my voice. I mean, really, which Head of State would take that chance? Don't they always have all kinds of police escorts and secret service people swarming around them like bees in a hive? But Adamson was emphatic.

"Is true. I heard a story dat one time he was travelling along de road where some soldiers were collecting bribes from motorists and putting de money in a box. J. J. was in de traffic watching dem collecting de money and stashing it in de box. While de soldiers were busy questioning some people, J. J. left his car and went over and took de box of money. The next day, de two soldiers were gone. No longer soldiers."

We cruised along the hot parched road to Kumasi, passing through many small towns. About three hours into our journey, we entered a quaint little town, crowded with shoppers. A saliva-inducing aroma of freshly baked bread wafted through the warm country air. A slight breeze rustled the trees lining our path. Crude wooden tables lined the street. Arranged on the makeshift tables were stout, slightly-brown breads, baked to perfection. The cookie-cutter breads were stacked uniformly on all the tables like little pyramids, each a duplicate of the other. The vendors, young women and men, stood behind the tables waiting for shoppers to relieve them of their products. We drove for almost a mile seeing nothing but bread! My salivary glands sprang into action, but when I observed that the breads were unwrapped, exposing them to the elements, I quickly coerced them back to normalcy.

We were in the centre of the town when without any warning, the traffic froze. Good, I thought, I'll take some pictures of the bread tables. Adamson had driven too quickly for me to capture a memory of the sites. I whipped out the little camera from my purse, ready to snap. Suddenly, like a strong wind rippling through a cornfield, there was rustling among the crowd on the street. Something dramatic must be happening, I thought. Fear gripped me. What if it's a street fight and we were caught up in the middle of it? Would we be caught in the cross-fire? I craned my neck to see what the commotion was about, only to see the crowd surging toward us from the opposite side of the street.

"What is it Adamson? What's going on?" my voice had a frightened edge.

Adamson grinned as he looked at me, "Just a minute, you'll soon see."

"See what? Are you going to sit here and let us be stampeded to death?" There was no denying the panic in my voice.

"Relax Ashanti woman!" Adamson grinned again.

I turned to look at him directly, then from the corner of my eye I saw the reason. Moving slowly toward us, was a shiny white car, dozens of people hanging on while others ran behind it. One would have thought they'd never seen a car before. Through the windows, which were wide open, I saw what was causing the commotion. A bride and groom! She, gorgeous in a white dress and veil, grinned happily as she waved at the crowd. He, in a dark suit, smiled and waved frantically at the people. The car drove slowly through the town with the crowd following for several metres, then it picked up speed and disappeared out of sight. As freshly baked bread was the forte of the little town, I dubbed it the bread town and to this day can still smell the pleasant aroma that teased my nostrils.

— ◇ —

Many interesting sights caught my attention along the way but there was one which fascinated me most. At several points young men held up dead animals the size of a mongoose. Some had the animals tied to sticks by the legs then hoisted over their shoulders while others held the animals upside down by the legs. They offered to sell the dead animals to passers-by.

"What on earth is that?" I asked after we'd passed a few.

"Oh, dat's a Grass Cutter!" Adamson said as he smacked his lips. He seemed pretty excited.

"A Grass Cutter? That's the name of the animal?"

"Yes, dat is the sweetest meat you could ever eat."

"No way would I eat that thing. It looks like a bloody rat!" I retorted.

"Wait until you try it," Adamson said in his deep African drawl.

"Never!"

The mere thought of eating meat from that animal sent my stomach in a tail spin. And yet, here was Adamson salivating over it. Culture and upbringing is the single most powerful thing in one's life.

It defines who we are, what we'll do and where we'll go. For a brief moment, I was ready to condemn Adamson, to ridicule him, then I thought about escargots. It was something I'd sworn would never pass my lips. Who the heck wants to eat snails? I'd asked with disgust the first time it was introduced to me. Now it's a great delicacy that I enjoy! I kept quiet after that.

Farther along the road, I saw mounds of red clay shaped like miniature mountains. They reminded me of tiny versions of the Piton mountains in St. Lucia. My initial thoughts were that someone was experimenting with clay, for some of the mounds were about six feet high. After we passed about a dozen of them, curiosity got the better of me.

"Adamson, what are those little clay mountains? I've seen a few so far."

Adamson took his eyes off the road to look at me.

"You never see dose before?"

"No, I don't know what they are."

"Dey are ant hills."

Adamson smiled. It was a smile that said I have one up on you, Yvonne. It was now his turn to teach a woman of the world something.

"You are putting me on!"

"Putting yuh on?" Adamson asked with wide-eyed innocence.

I kept forgetting he is not familiar with some of my slang expressions.

"I mean, is this really true? Those large hills are made by ants?"

I was awestruck. They looked like mini mountains jutting out of the earth, in varying stages of construction. Sometimes they were in groups, other times they were solitary. They must be some enormous ants, I thought. I couldn't envisage such tiny creatures building those structures.

"Yeah, de soldier ants build dem. Dere is a colony of ants inside, and it has a queen ant," Adamson replied.

"Can you stop so I can take a picture of the next one?"

"Sure, no problem."

Adamson seemed amused at my wonderment. I didn't care, I just wanted a picture of what seemed to be a strange phenomenon.

— ◇ —

We arrived in Kumasi in the early afternoon, and Adamson asked a man at the side of the road for directions to the Stadium Hotel. He spoke in *Twi*, one of the Ashanti dialect, and the stranger responded in the same language.

"How come you can speak the Ashanti language?" I asked.

"I pick it up by listening to dem."

"You mean no one ever taught you?"

"No, when you hang out wid dem you can pick it up easy."

He never ceased to amaze me.

Humphrey, the hotel receptionist in Accra, had recommended the Stadium Hotel in Kumasi. It was located close to the town and a few blocks away from Kumasi's huge stadium. The structure was one you couldn't overlook. The old rustic two-storey building was alive with character, dominating the quiet, secluded street. We barely squeezed into the tiny parking lot that had been further reduced by a pile of building supplies. The material was being used to complete renovations of the hotel's restaurant which were well underway.

At the reception desk the clerk handed me the price list and I looked it over.

"We would like to have a look at your single and double rooms please," I said.

He led us up a flight of stairs, to the right, and through a set of double doors. The single room was small, dowdy, and uninviting. The double room didn't seem much better. It contained one queen-size bed.

"I don't think any of these will suit us. Can we see one of your suites?" The appearance of the rooms was not complimentary to the stature of the hotel.

"No problem Miss, I'll get the keys."

He scurried down the stairs and returned with another set of keys jingling in his hand.

"Come this way please."

He led us to the other side of the stairs on the same floor. The suite looked brighter, with a pair of twin beds separated by a night table, a mahogany dressing table, and double closets. The long, narrow bathroom had hot and cold water, a tub and all the other amenities. The suite had a small sitting room with windows looking out toward a

corridor. There were two double seat couches, a coffee table, a colour
TV, a small refrigerator and a Ghetto Blaster.

"This looks much better," I said.

Out of earshot of the clerk, I said to Adamson "I hope you don't
mind if we share a suite?"

"Of course not, I tink it would be too expensive to get two
separate rooms," he said.

Back at the lobby, I told the clerk we would take the suite.

He sent the Bellboy to the room with our luggage. We followed
him and after he left, Adamson and I had a chance to sit back and relax
after our long journey.

At the first opportunity, I called Abu, Paddy's Kumasi associate.
He sounded pleased to hear from me.

"I would love to meet you and talk with you," he said on the
phone. "But I have been sick with the malaria since December. I have
not even been to work since December."

Malaria! Wild thoughts raced through my mind. I've never known
anyone with that tropical disease before, and secondly, I hadn't received
any malaria shots for this trip. Before the trip to Africa, I called the
Tropical Disease Centre in Toronto, and a recorded message said the
malaria alert was over in West Africa. I interpreted that to mean no
malaria treatment was required. Now it seemed the disease was
around. I hesitated to accept Abu's invitation fearing I might catch it.
I hadn't come this far to catch any tropical disease that would deter me
from my mission. I was about to decline Abu's offer when my high
school biology lessons kicked in. Malaria is not a virus you contract, you
get it from being bitten by the female anopheles mosquito. I felt
relieved.

"Sure, I'd love to visit you," I replied.

"I will send my driver to pick you up. Where are you staying?"

"I'm at the Stadium hotel."

"Can you be ready in, say, half an hour?"

"Sure, I'll be ready."

While Adamson showered and took a nap, Abu's driver whisked
me away in his master's four-wheel-drive Grand Cherokee! Abu lived
on a hill which commanded a spectacular view of the city of Kumasi.
The area was strictly residential and contained several large houses. I
surmised it must be where some of the wealthy Ashantis live.

As we pulled into the driveway of Abu's house, the front door burst open, and Abu welcomed me with open arms. I felt like a long-lost sister returning home, like the prodigal daughter. Any moment I expected him to order the fatted calf to be prepared for feasting. I couldn't have felt more welcomed if I were his blood relative. While he hugged me closely, tears welled up in my eyes. I squinted to hold them back, not wanting to embarrass myself. It was about the sixth time since arriving in Ghana that I was overcome with emotions. It was one of those feelings which comes from your innards, but you know not whence it comes and whither it goes. Everywhere I visited, I experienced the same warm feeling of belonging, a difficult thing to explain, but easier to understand. The Ghanaian word for greeting is *akwaaba*, but it doesn't just mean welcome, it also means, come join us. In my case, the word *akwaaba* was quite real and very much alive.

Abu led me into a spacious living room which looked out onto an elevated dining room. He introduced me to three of his co-workers who were visiting. They welcomed me with enthusiasm. One fellow was about five feet tall, wore round wire-rim glasses and looked like the nerdy type.

"You look like the brains of this group," I said as I smiled at him. Everyone laughed and nodded.

"He is our computer whiz," Abu said.

"See, just as I thought, he is the brains," I said.

They asked me a few questions about Canada which I eagerly answered. Shortly after my arrival the tallest of the three stood up. It seemed they'd visited long enough for he said,

"Let us pray for brother Abu before we go."

Everyone stood and closed their eyes. So not wanting to be the odd one out, I did the same. The prayer asked that "Brother Abu" recovers soon, and a blessing for the visitor to enjoy herself in Ghana and return home safely. All during the prayer I kept thinking that this man must be a lay preacher, he was so articulate. When the prayer ended all three said their goodbyes and departed.

Abu and I were now alone, giving me a chance to study him more. He was an attractive man, medium built and slightly greying at the temples. He smiled at me with such warmth; his smile could melt an ice cube.

"Sister Yvonne, are you sure you're not from here? You look so familiar." Abu gazed into my eyes.

"I guess I am, indirectly," I said.

We both laughed. Abu knew to what I alluded.

"There is no doubt that most of the black West Indians came from this part of the world. Everywhere I've been, the people look exactly like West Indians."

"Well, I'm sure you know the history. Many of the slaves who were shipped to the West Indies, came from West Africa with many from The Gold Coast, now Ghana."

"You never know Abu, you and I could be blood relatives," I teased. Abu looked at me and smiled.

"I wouldn't mind that at all, Yvonne," he said. Then on a more serious note, he asked, "So tell me about Canada and this Quebec business. Are they going to separate?"

I was taken off guard. I never thought Africans took any interest in such a Canadian political issue. Quebec, a province with a quarter of the population, had lost the vote to separate from the rest of Canada in a 1995 referendum by a very close margin. It hadn't stopped the ongoing debate between Quebec and the rest of Canada, and arguments had heated up somewhat in recent months. I gave him my views on the subject, and we went on to talk about various other topics. Abu was obviously a very well-read man. He spoke knowingly on several topical issues. I enjoyed the discussion as this was the calibre of conversation I loved. While we talked, I kept blowing and wiping my dripping nose.

"I must apologize for this cold, Abu. You know, I haven't had one in four years and here I am in Ghana only five days, and already I have a cold. What do you think of that?" Abu gave a hearty laugh from deep within his chest.

"Don't worry about it, Yvonne, at least it is not malaria!"

"Thank God," I said.

"It's a disease you don't want to get."

"How does the malaria make you feel?"

"You feel weak, no energy. When I stand up, I feel like my legs are going to buckle under me."

A friend of Abu's dropped by and was introduced. Charles was the architect who had built Abu's house and three houses next to it. This was the sort of camaraderie that I didn't have in Canada, and one that

I missed. I loved to have friends drop in just as Charles did. This is the way it used to be in the Caribbean. You could always drop in unannounced at a friend's home, knowing that you would always be welcomed. You never had to call ahead or make an appointment, and when you showed up, you never had to apologize for being there. Charles was obviously comfortable dropping in on Abu, and Abu was happy to see him. This is a part of what brotherhood is all about.

"Great work," I said as I turned my head and looked around "This is a lovely house."

The design was similar to many of the upscale houses in the Caribbean, made from sturdy concrete bricks. It was painted pale pink, with a flat roof and redwood louvre shutters.

"Thank you. This was built four years ago," Charles said.

"You should see some of his great work; this is nothing."

Abu praised his friend who seemed very modest for he held his head down, bashfully, then changed the subject.

We had a lively conversation going when Abu's servant served light refreshments. I saw no evidence of a wife, and I wondered if Abu was married. He obviously enjoyed my company and was disappointed that I planned to return to Accra the next afternoon. We said a warm goodbye to each other, and Abu's driver returned me to my hotel.

I knew that had I planned to stay longer in Kumasi, I would have gotten to know Abu really well, but it was not to be.

A S H A N T I !

*A*fter Adamson and I dined at a quaint little restaurant, nestled among the shops in the heart of Kumasi, we drove around the town. I wanted a nocturnal view the city. If there were cocooning nights in Kumasi it was obviously not on Fridays. The city bustled with many people walking about, greeting each other, talking, and laughing making it a happy place. Adamson stopped the car on a side street, parking it as close to the curb as he could.

"Hey Adamson, that looks like an interesting bar over there," I said, pointing to a building across the street with flickering lights.

"It look okay, want to go in?" He looked at me curiously.

"Sure, why not? We can at least have a drink."

We scuttled across the road, looking out for crazy drivers. Soon we were swallowed up in the crowd of patrons. The place emanated a feeling of friendship and camaraderie. Through the bustle, sounds of glasses clinking, bottle caps scattering on the floor, and cans popping as they released pressure, a waitress led us to a table for two where we parked tired bodies on smooth wooden chairs. I ordered a Guilder beer while Adamson ordered non-alcoholic malt.

"Well, here's to Kumasi," I said, lifting my glass and clinking it against Adamson's bottle.

"Here's to yuh, Ashanti woman! Dis is your town." He looked into my eyes penetratingly.

"And here's to you Hausa man!" I said, grinning as I was caught up in the moment. We clinked glass and bottle again. Slowly, we sipped our drinks, savouring it as we took in the scene. Adamson said hello to a few people and I smiled and nodded when eyes met mine. When we finished our drinks, I touched Adamson on his arm,

"Let's follow the example of the locals, and walk about the town."

"Are yuh sure? How's yuh cold?" His voice was tender and he seemed concerned.

"Oh, don't worry. It's a hot night, the fresh air will do me good."

We walked about aimlessly for a while and before we knew it, we'd climbed a steep hill where we found a natural lockout point. We looked over the sprawling city with lights glimmering in the night like tiny stars. I looked up at the sky, a thick, purple, velvet blanket dotted with twinkling stars. It was a celestial glory. Hot tropical air warmed our faces while the perfumed tropical smell of the land engulfed us. We watched shadowy movements of people below. My ears picked up the barely audible night sounds of crickets chirping, accompanied by frogs croaking from distant bushes. How serene and peaceful it all seemed from our high vantage point. Why oh why, can't the world be at peace, I mused. The serenity led me to thinking about my busy lifestyle in Toronto, one that afforded me little time out to admire the stars and to be at peace with the universe. I pondered the magnificent world in which we live, and became lost in the mystery of it all. I wondered if the stars I was looking at were the same ones seen on rare occasions when I looked up into the Canadian sky. At that moment, I decided star gazing was something worth pursuing. I would embark on a new adventure on my return home.

Before heading back to our hotel, we stopped to have another drink at the bar we'd visited earlier. Half way through our drinks I sneezed three consecutive times. Adamson looked into my watering eyes, and shook his head.

"I know yuh shouldn't take dat walk. Let us go back to de hotel right now."

He left me no room to argue. He quickly paid the bill against my feeble protest, and we headed for the car.

We arrived at our hotel around 10:00 p.m. and I couldn't wait to shower and flop into bed. By then, the head cold had taken away most of my energy, and my breathing became labourious.

I lay on the first bed trying to sleep. The air conditioner was going full blast, making a loud hum. I watched the ceiling-fan circle slowly, around and around and around. I felt as if I were revolving with it, as if any moment, I would fall off the bed. My nose became stuffier and stuffier and my body felt hot to the touch. I suspected I had a fever. The trip to Kumasi had been a long tiring one and Adamson's hot car with no air-conditioning, had made it even more exhausting.

But it wasn't just tiredness and the head cold that kept me awake.

Something else was blocking sleep. Something else was disturbing my thoughts. I wanted to hide from it, fabricate excuses, philosophize, moralize, but it was no use pretending; I knew what it was, I was sharing a suite with a young man. Over the past five days, this young man had been with me constantly. We'd spent almost every waking moment together. He'd become a part of my daily routine. Lying in one bed, knowing that within minutes Adamson would be in the next bed, and so close was distracting. I began to wish that he would sleep on one of the couches in the sitting room. Would it be unreasonable to ask him to do so? If he asked why, what would I say to him?

At thirty-four, he was virile. When I'd asked him if he was involved with anyone, he'd made it clear that it was too early after his wife's death, that he'd not looked at another woman. From all indications, he was obviously infatuated with me. I would have to be blind not to notice it. As the days wore on, I'd observed a certain shyness about him, a shyness which wasn't there before. I saw the way he looked deep into my eyes when we sat opposite each other, and how he held onto every word I spoke.

I'd ignored it. Several times he'd expressed his fascination for me.

"I never met anyone like yuh before," he'd said.

"What do you mean?"

"You can do anyting, go anywhere without asking anyone?"

"Sure, I make my own decisions. I don't need permission from anyone."

Little did he know that not only did I make my own decisions, I also made important decisions for many people. I'd deliberately withheld information about myself from him. He'd no detail about my job or my life. He managed to glean that I worked for a bank but he didn't know what I did.

He was very impressed with my independence, and amazed that I could do anything I wanted without consulting anyone. I wondered how different his idea of how a woman should behave must be, compared to mine. I'd grown to like Adamson, liked him a lot. He was assertive, friendly and fun to be with, but I'd never thought of him in a romantic way. Sure he was handsome. He had a physique that when he walked into a room, women took a second glance. His innocence, like unspoilt chastity fascinated me, but he was not my type. After all, he was only a few years older than my daughter, and I didn't regard myself as a cradle robber.

Besides, what did we have in common except skin colour? Not a lot. But I was a healthy woman who had had no physical contact with a man for a long time. Since arriving in Ghana, occasional feelings of desire had zipped through my body, but I'd chalked them up to the steaming Ghanaian sun! I had no designs on anyone, and certainly my trip had nothing to do with me seeking romance. My trip to Africa was to fulfill a dream, a burning desire, to see the land of my ancestors.

As I lay tossing and turning I asked myself, how will I feel if Adamson were to make a pass at me? I wasn't sure how I should react, and I most certainly didn't want to hurt his feelings. Do I say, "Young man, don't be ridiculous, go to your bed?" Or, "I'm flattered that you feel this way, but I couldn't do anything of the sort?" In the height of my contemplation, an inner voice cautioned, "Yvonne, the young man is not lusting after your body; he only sees you as you are, a nice friendly person."

An hour later, still wide awake, I was fresh out of scenarios, when Adamson entered the bedroom.

"You're not sleeping yet?" he asked as he peered at me in the semi darkness.

"No, I think we'll have to turn off the air-conditioning, it's too noisy and besides, I'm feeling chilly." I pulled the crisp white sheet up under my chin. Chilly was a mild way to describe how I felt. Goose bumps covered my entire body. My nipples jutted through the white cotton night gown, hard as board, hurting from taut skin. Adamson promptly switched off the air-conditioning and fan.

"Let me feel your forehead." He came over to my bed and placed the back of his hand on my forehead. "I tink yuh have a fever. Do yuh have any medicine?"

"I have some Tylenol in my bag on the dresser. Would you bring me the bag please?"

He brought the bag and I rummaged through it and found the pills. He fetched me a glass of water from the small refrigerator and I downed two pills. After that he tucked me in, the way I used to do with my son.

"Please try to get some rest now—good night," he said softly. He moved to the other side of the room. I watched him discreetly as he took off his shirt, then attempted to slide under the sheets still wearing his pants and belt.

"Adamson, don't tell me you are sleeping in your clothes! Take off your pants; they will be crushed tomorrow if you sleep in them!" I sounded like a mother talking to her teenage son. It was obvious that he was shy and not quite sure what to do. Hesitantly, he removed his pants and belt, leaving his shorts on, then he slid under the sheets into the other bed.

But try as I may, I couldn't fall asleep. After another hour of tossing and turning I slid over, onto Adamson's bed and put my head on his chest.

"Adamson, I hope you don't mind me resting on you. I feel so cold," I whispered in the still of the night. My lips were chapped and every muscle in my body ached.

"No, I don't mind, I was awake. I'm glad yuh came over," he whispered back.

With the airconditioner and fan switched off, you could've heard a cotton ball bounce off the floor. The only thing audible, was Adamson's heart pounding in his chest, each beat faster than the one before. I inhaled the fresh sensuous Hugo Boss cologne he always wore, even with my stuffy nose. He must have dabbed some on after he had his shower. I wanted to bury my nose in his muscular chest. Suddenly, a feeling of loneliness engulfed me. I wanted to be held, to feel strong protective arms around me. Fear enveloped my body. Suppose I'd caught malaria? What if what I had wasn't a simple cold but some terrible tropical disease? I wanted the warmth of Adamson's body to take my chill away. My heartbeat began to compete with Adamson's, and before long, I was sure mine had outpaced his. He put his arms around me nervously, at first, then he squeezed me tightly. Within seconds, like osmosis, I felt his body warmth transmitted to mine.

I awoke next morning to the sound of roosters crowing and birds twittering. For a moment I was disoriented. I thought I'd woken up in Jamaica, in the small town of Newport where I grew up. The nostalgia of my childhood came flooding back. My mind wandered to the early mornings when roosters, or cocks as we called them, would crow just as they were doing now. It seemed at about 5:00 a.m. each morning, one cock would start the chain reaction. He would give a wailing cock-ah-doodle-do, then all the other cocks in the neighbourhood would respond. Within minutes every rooster within earshot was crowing one after the other. It was like an orchestra with each section crowing a part. The poorer farmers, including my grandparents, were awakened each morning by this kind of wake-up call. Cocks were their alarm clocks and they never ran out of batteries nor needed winding.

Whenever I had to wake up early, grandmother used to say, "Before cock put on his drawers, you better get up." I didn't have to decipher that command. I knew wake-up time would be at the first cockcrow. I envisioned the morning dew on the tall grass, and as it formed on large, green coco leaves. Glistening droplets spiralled down the groves, formed by the main vein of the leaves, before dripping onto the ground. Farmers often had to wear goulashes, the dew was so heavy.

The twittering of birds was also a wonderful part of my childhood. The old family homestead stood poised on a hill surrounded by several acres of land on which fruit trees abounded. All kinds of birds darted about from branch to branch gathering worms or whatever else they ate in the early mornings. There were Grassquits, Pitcheries, Ground Doves, Bald Pearts, and several other names which were obviously not biological names. However, those were the names we knew, their chirping forever sweet music to my ears. And ahhh, the aromatic, perfumed smell of coffee and citrus blossoms. It drove busybody honey bees crazy as they buzzed from one small, white flower to the other, gathering the powdery, yellow pollen from the centres.

Lying in bed in Kumasi, I was experiencing a flash back!

Filled with contentment, I stretched, and yawned. I felt young and sensuous. It was great to be alive, to be in a place I'd never known before, to experience what must be common place for the Ashanti people. I looked around the strange room and rocketed back to reality when I saw Adamson sitting on his bed staring at me.

"I been watching yuh for half hour and hoping yuh would wake up," he said.

"Well I'm up now. I had a fantastic dream."

"Was I in dere?" he asked with wide-eyed innocence.

"That, you'll never know," I said, grinning at him.

Adamson decided he would play the role of doctor. "I'm going to take yuh to Kumasi Market to find some medicine to get rid of yuh cold quick," he said.

I did not object; I desperately wanted to be rid of it.

On the streets of Kumasi, we witnessed a bright, sunny Saturday morning as all the days had been since my arrival in Ghana. Today, it seemed brighter, sunnier, or was it all in my head? Adamson seemed less talkative. We drove into town and he parked the car close to some stores on a steep incline. While Accra seemed to be fairly flat, Kumasi was hilly. Hundreds of people moved about the town. Kumasi's battered taxis were everywhere. One could spot them easily, as they were all painted green and yellow. Similar to Accra, every second car in Kumasi was a Peugeot. The French car manufacturer certainly had the automobile market sewn up in Ghana. From all appearances, they were in for a windfall very soon, for most of the cars were old and battered. Before long, thousands of them would have to be replaced. After two days in the country, I'd stopped feeling badly about Adamson's car. His looked good compared to many I'd seen on the roads. I imagined those cars being crushed flat and forming a part of landfills if they were in Canada.

We walked about a block to a wall overlooking a ledge. We gazed into the valley below and an unbelievable spectacle glared at us. As far as the eye could see were rambling shacks covered with pieces of dilapidated canvas or rusty zinc roofs. I couldn't take my eyes from the scene. It appeared like a giant honey comb, a large canvas of moving colours painted from the multicoloured clothing worn by hundreds of shoppers moving about, like worker bees, intertwined with shabby canvas coverings.

This was Kumasi Market!

Far beyond the shacks the city's skyline crested the horizon with tall church steeples, dotted with huge houses on hillsides, office buildings and two-storey commercial buildings.

Adamson led me into the valley like a lamb to the slaughter. As we moved amongst the people, he inquired where medicine could be found. He spoke in *Twi*, and the shoppers responded in the same dialect. Everyone he asked for direction, sent us further and further into the heart of the market.

Every conceivable product could be found in one or other of the stalls. There was fish, raw meat, onions, utensils, clothing, you name it, and it could be found there. Yams the size of massive jack-o-lantern pumpkins were stacked six feet into the air. I never knew they could be so large. When I thought about the yams my grandparents cultivated, they were tiny in comparison to Kumasi yams. In some areas, dirty water ran through shallow gutters, while the ground was strewn with rotting fruits and vegetables. The smell of burnt meat sifted through the air, while vendors young, old and in between, sat in their stalls oblivious to the smell.

While we trudged through the moving crowd I held onto Adamson's hand as if my life depended on it. I knew if I became detached, I would've become hysterical. Finally, we found the area where medicine was sold.

Adamson bought a lump of a soft yellow substance and the vendor, a plump middle-age woman with her head wrapped with a red cotton cloth, placed it in a clear plastic bag. He also bought a rub, a small tin container which looked similar to Vicks Vapour Rub.

Once Adamson secured the medicine, we began to move forward to try to get out of the market. We'd travelled some distance when we realized that instead of getting out, we were getting in deeper and deeper. We were lost! Adamson became annoyed with his performance as a guide; I consoled him not to be. After all, he was not from that city, and he didn't know his way around. He asked several people to show us the way out. We followed their directions and finally we were at the other side of the ledge where we first viewed the market. Our car was a quarter mile to our left. I thought we'd travelled straight ahead but it seemed we'd unwittingly veered to the west.

— ✧ —

While we sat in the car in the hellish heat, Adamson told me what to do. "Put some of de yellow stuff in yuh nose."

He spoke in a soft, gentle tone, as if he were speaking to a child. He handed me the plastic bag with the gooey looking stuff.

"Can't it wait until we get back to the hotel?" I asked. I didn't want to be seen with yellow goog dripping from my nose.

"No, yuh put it in now." His voice altered from soft to stern.

I eyed the bag, "What is it anyway?" I observed that the stuff was beginning to melt from the near-noonday heat.

"It's cocoa butter. Yuh know de cocoa tree? We passed some on de way here."

"Yes, I know cocoa, we have it in Jamaica." I was relieved knowing that chocolate was made from seeds of the cocoa fruit. At least my nose wouldn't disintegrate! "This had better be good," I said as I complied.

He handed me the small tin container.

"Rub yuh temples with this and put a little under yuh tongue. Yuh cold will soon be gone." His voice exuded confidence.

I looked at the substance in the tightly packed tin. It looked like Vaseline.

"Okay, Doctor, I'll do as you say," I said with resignation.

I followed his instructions precisely then checked with my compact mirror to make sure I didn't look like a creature from Mars.

The rest of the day we spent touring Kumasi. It's an old city with streets lined with two-storey buildings which housed stores, small shops, in front of which sidewalk vendors sold their wares. The city's population is about four hundred thousand, but the Ashanti region, the most populous of all Ghana, has over two million people. We visited the Cultural Centre, Zoo, and finally, the piece de resistance, the Ashanti Palace.

When some of my clients had concluded that my trip to Africa entailed going on a safari, I'd smiled, knowing that adventure wasn't in my plans. Visiting the zoo was therefore the best I could do to compensate. I'd accepted Adamson's recommendation to visit Kumasi's zoo with great anticipation. A more appropriate name for the zoo would've been "The Bat Zoo" or "Dracula's Hide-A-Way." Why the strange names you ask? When Adamson and I entered the zoo's main gate a wilderness of bats greeted us. Big, black bats hung upside-down from several large trees and from electrical wires. Some lay on the ground, dying, or dead. They were everywhere. I'd never seen a bat close-up before, for in the past, when I saw one, it flitted by quickly. Here, a field of black bats dominated a part of the zoo. I can't say they were attractive creatures and the connotation of blood, death, and Dracula didn't help me to appreciate them. I asked Adamson to let us move on quickly. Not only were the bats a turnoff, the rest of the zoo took us by surprise.

Thinking of the zoo as a mini safari, I expected to see many exotic animals, animals indigenous to Ghana and other African countries. I also expected to see healthy, well-attended animals. Instead I saw forlorn specimens in dilapidated surroundings, where the grass grew tall and the paths were shabby. One animal caught my interest however, it was the Kotoko. I'd never seen or heard of this animal before, and it's difficult to describe. A black and white hairy creature the size of a beaver, it had a beautiful tail, similar to that of a squirrel. It stared at me with unblinking eyes through the wooden bars of its cage. I took a photograph of it but the bars of the cage obstructed the shot, causing the animal to be almost invisible when the picture was later developed. Except for playful monkeys, and a few other well known animals, there wasn't much more to see. The poor condition of the grounds didn't encourage us to spend much time and I left feeling very disappointed.

After a late lunch, we arrived at the gates of the Ashanti Palace. The entrance fee was five thousand cedis for tourists and two thousand cedis for locals. I couldn't understand the differentiation in pricing based on those lines, but I paid it and Adamson and I joined a group who was waiting for the next tour to begin. It commenced with a viewing of the palanquins which were used to transport the king and his family. Some of the colourful, upholstered carriages with soft linings were hundreds of years old. Kings were lifted above the crowd and carried manually in their carriages. After that the curator led us into the main building.

The palace was truly impressive, both in structure, and even more so for the contents. We entered a large two storey building with many rooms, first seeing a spacious living room that was filled with paraphernalia and photographs showing numerous heads of states who had visited the palace. Reigning King Otumfuo Opoku Ware II, well entrenched in his role, was into the twenty seventh year of his reign, having celebrated his twenty fifth anniversary in 1995. We asked if he was there and were told we had to make an appointment before we could see him. One Caucasian American tourist with the group ahead of us was annoyed that she couldn't see the king, and wanted to know why she had to make an appointment. As she pouted and swore, I thought, how totally arrogant. Would she drive up to Buckingham Palace in London and demand to see the queen and expect Queen Elizabeth II to receive her just like that? Or would she arrive at the White House in Washington and expect to see the President without an appointment? Why should the Ashanti king be treated any differently? I supposed in her mind, the Ashanti king wasn't a real king. I left her fuming as we continued the tour, smiling a little to myself.

The curator who guided us was wonderful with a good sense of humour. Our tour group was small including Adamson, two Germans, (one spoke no English, his friend translated everything we said) an

Englishman and myself. At one stage we entered a large room where walls were lined with huge paintings, all portraits of King Otumfuo. Most of the paintings were done by university students. Being an art lover, I began to scrutinize each painting while moving along the walls, oblivious to the direction the rest of the group took. While some were rather amateurish, others were true to the king's photographs. Soon I had moved half way across the large room.

"Excuse me Miss, are you conducting this tour now?"

The curator's voice boomed across at me. I looked back to see him and the rest of the tour group laughing at me. Smiling at the insinuation, I promptly rejoined them. The curator was undoubtedly very knowledgable. I told him that my forefathers were Ashantis and he looked at me curiously while his eyes lit up.

"Do you know which village they came from? If you know this, it will be easy for us to trace your roots."

Tracing my roots? This is incredible. I could find out who my real ancestors were, where they came from and what they did. All the curiosity stored inside me, like good wine could come of age! Had the time come for tasting? Oh, what a bonus this would be! But alas, I felt my disappointment deeply for I'd never known the name of the village. When I planned the trip to Ghana, I had no plans to trace my roots. Being in the country of my ancestors was enough for me. But if I could only trace my roots ....

"If I'd known this could be done, and so easily, I would have done some research before my trip! Oh darn, I'm missing a great opportunity," I said, sighing with disappointment.

"Don't feel bad my dear, you're not the first to feel this way. Maybe next time?" He smiled as he patted my arm.

Adamson hadn't exaggerated when he told me about Ashanti gold. Some of the ornaments and jewellery, or replicas thereof, which were worn by the king and members of the royal court were displayed in the palace. The king wore gold ornaments from head to toe. Our curator pointed out that on ceremonial occasions when he's dressed in all his gold pieces, he is almost immobilised by their weight. There's even a golden stool with a fascinating legend.

As the story goes, the Golden Stool was conjured up out of the sky in 1701, by the chief priest of Osei Tutu, the first leader of the Ashanti empire. In 1896, after more than twenty years of war with the

British, the Ashantis were finally defeated, but they hid the Golden Stool. It resurfaced in 1921. It is so sacred to the Ashantis that no one, including the king, must ever sit on it. It is placed on its own chair next to the King during ceremonies.

The gold displayed at the palace was the Real McCoy. Nothing like the flimsy mixed alloy stuff we purchase in jewellery stores at home. This was solid gold—cast gold. I stared at the pieces in amazement as I realized their monetary as well as spiritual values.

Farther along the tour the curator ushered us into another room where he made a grand announcement. "This is the moment you've been waiting for." We stood tense, waiting. "I know you've all wanted to see His Majesty."

We waited with bated breath to see the great one.

"Here is the King!" With the poise of a ringmaster, he audaciously, unveiled a life-size photograph of King Otumfuo Opoku Ware II, dressed in all his splendour.

The group burst into hysterical laughter. After we calmed down and dried our eyes, and the curator regained his composure, he explained that the king was not on the premises that day.

A short while later, I thought the curator had lied to us, and almost jumped out of my skin when I saw the King sitting in one of the rooms. But alas, it was only an effigy, extremely lifelike but still not what we wanted to see. Several effigies of members of the royal court were arranged around the room. The quality was superb. Every detail including wrinkles, kinky hair, and skin colour was duplicated. Madame Tussaud's work couldn't come close to this marvellous Ashanti art.

The Ashanti Palace is a place I'll treasure for a long time. The exposure to some of the missing pieces of my heritage, pieces I was unaware to be missing, was mind boggling. The fact that this revelation all came about by the sheer coincidence of meeting Adamson was also a mystery. Many times during the days as I toured Accra, I asked myself the question, "What if?" What if I hadn't met the unknown stranger at the airport upon my arrival? What if I'd never met Adamson? Was my trip here alive with serendipity? It was difficult to envisage the success of my visit without knowing Adamson. He'd become so much a part of my daily life, at times he was like the air I breathed. Gaining first-hand knowledge of the life and history of the Ashantis, had a special meaning for me. I thanked Adamson over and over again for taking me to the wonderful place called Kumasi. It made be doubly proud to know that I am associated with such outstanding, colourful people, that some trace of Ashanti blood flows through my veins.

After we left the Ashanti palace, we drove to Kumasi's prison where Adamson's sister worked as a warden. The two-storey concrete building with decorative brick walls on the second floor, somehow, didn't seem as foreboding as some prisons I've seen. But it was the statue in the centre of the round-a-bout opposite the prison that caught my attention. A large male lion with a curly tail, looking much like Mufasa from *The Lion King*, stood regally on a pedestal surrounded by a cluster of green shrubs with tiny yellow flowers. Standing on top of the lion was a thin, tall man. He was bare chested except for a scarf around his neck. From his waist to ankle, he was clothed in a mustard coloured wrap-a-round skirt. Holding a cup and a towel, he seemed to be in the throes of praying or performing a ritual.

"Adamson!" I called, pointing at the statue, "What's that all about?" By now I'd learned that many of the statues were depictions of legends.

"Dat one is about a famous lion dat used to terrorize de village. It killed many people and no one could catch it. One day, dey got a medicine man to use his power. He use his potion to calm the lion and dey were able to catch it. Dat's the medicine man on top of de lion." He looked at the statue admiringly. Whatever became of guns, I wondered.

Adamson inquired about Mary at the prison gate and learned that she had left work for the day. We drove directly to her apartment to find her preparing supper in the backyard. Her husband had taken their three-year-old daughter for a walk and they returned just in time for supper.

Their apartment building was a ramshackle two storey structure which begged for maintenance. I was shocked when Adamson said it was housing provided by the government. It made me wonder what housing for the poor must be like. I dared not allow my imagination to run wild. The kitchen was a separate building just behind the apartment, but this evening Mary wasn't cooking in the kitchen. Cooking was taking place smack in the centre of the backyard between the apartment building and the kitchen. On the ground secured between three stones, an open fire burned brightly, flames occasionally leaping into the air. A pot bubbled and spluttered with froth streaming over the sides. Mary organized other dishes on a low table nearby. Neighbours on either side, were also preparing meals outdoors. I watched with interest as two teenage girls pounded yams close by. Boiled yams were placed in a large mortar. Each girl had a five-foot wooden stick which was smooth and rounded like a baseball bat. They pounded the bottom of the stick into the mortar. One rammed into the mortar, then the other, back and forth they alternated in rhythm. When the pounding was finished, the dough-like yam was placed in a large bowl. Mary offered us supper which consisted of the pounded yam, and a tasty soup with bits of chicken in it. Although pounded yams looked similar to fu-fu, it is not as sticky, and I was able to chew it more easily. We chatted with Mary and her husband until after dinner, then Adamson and I bade them goodbye, and began our return trip to Accra.

The drive back was more leisurely. Having appeased my anxiety to see Kumasi, I relaxed and concentrated on the scenery, knowing that I would not pass that way again for a long time.

Halfway into our journey, I began to feel uncomfortable as I inhaled fumes from the car's exhaust. Not long after, the motor died. I then had the experience of watching Adamson's mechanical genius at work. While I sat on a stone, under a tree at the side of the road, he worked on the car doing what he could under the circumstances. Eventually, he managed to get the car started and to a place where he found a mechanic's shop. A pipe had to be welded together and once it was done, we were on our way again.

The jolly chatter and teasing which had taken place between Adamson and me during the trip to Kumasi, was noticeably absent. I was engrossed in my thoughts, reliving the night before when I curled up in his arms, when he'd brought warmth back to my body, remembering his passion and his plea, "I love yuh Yvonne; take me with yuh!"

I'd fallen off the magic carpet with a thud as realization hit me right smack in the centre of my forehead. The fever that had roasted my body, exited as if exorcized by an unknown spirit.

"Adamson, don't be ridiculous, you don't love me. That is impossible. I can't take you with me."

We talked some more and decided we would keep in touch.

How should I react to him now? What were his expectations?

I sensed Adamson was glancing at me but when I looked at him his eyes were glued to the road ahead. It was my guess he was going through a similar thought process. How would we react to each other now that the unspoken rule was broken?

I awoke Sunday morning in my hotel room after the long, return-trip from Kumasi. A frown began to take shape on my face like a slowly rising sun. I was puzzled that I felt so good. I no longer had a head cold. My nose that had spewed quarts of colourless mucus uncontrollably, was as dry as Kumasi's dusty roads. The question surfaced, should I believe in bush medicine? I always thought there was merit to it, but was never quite sure if it really worked. For example: the good old Jamaican remedy for a cold was a shot of our famous overproof white rum, said to be one hundred and fifty proof, mixed with honey and lime juice. I've used this remedy many times in Canada, to cure the many colds I used to get in the winters, and although I would get the sweats after ingesting it, the cold usually dragged on for three or four days. In the end, I'm not sure whether the cold ran its course or the remedy worked. There are several variations to this remedy in the Caribbean, but who knows if they really work.

On this lustrous Sunday morning, as I stretched, yawned and rolled out of bed, I was certain of one thing, there was no trace of the terrible head cold I'd suffered from. The miserable cold I had the day I left Kumasi was no more. Not a hint of a sniffle, nothing, zilch. Dr. Adamson Mone would have to be commended for his incredible prescription. I wanted to phone him as soon as I had breakfast.

GUARDIAN ANGEL

The first time I saw Suobite, I thought he was odd. Somehow, he didn't fit in with the other passengers sprawled around us. We were sitting in the sweltering Ghanaian heat in a semi-covered waiting area of Kotoka International Airport. It was a large square area lined with blue fibreglass chairs, arranged along three sides. The fourth side led directly through glass doors into the main ticket counter section of the airport. The temperature topped ninety-five degrees Fahrenheit. This part of the airport had no air-conditioning. If the architects, who built the structure, assumed that the fresh air which blew in through the open sides would make it cool enough, they were dead wrong.

I was dressed in a floral red, green, orange and yellow, short sleeve blouse with a matching ankle length skirt. My shoulder-length black shiny braid extensions, remained neat and fresh after ten days. So far, I'd blended in nicely with the native Africans. In fact, I realized for my purpose, that the braids were unnecessary since many African women now straightened their hair or sported geri-curls. Many wore makeup and dressed in the latest fashions, thus rendering my feeble attempt at a disguise a waste of time. There was just this one small thing that gave me away, my undeniable, irrefutable Canadian-Jamaican accent, when I spoke. Looking back at the love and acceptance, I received in Ghana, that too, was not a hindrance. But Nigeria? Who knows?

The heat was unbearable. I wanted to rip off my blouse exposing the yellow sleeveless tube top beneath. Salty perspiration trickled down my forehead to my nose and then splashed noiselessly into my lap. I felt drops of sweat running down my back. The tube top absorbed it. I retrieved a white, man-sized handkerchief from my purse, and mopped my face while I studied the other passengers. There were about fifty including four small children waiting for the 5:30 p.m. Nigerian Airways flight to Lagos. The children fidgeted, moving from one empty chair to another. Some ladies were dressed in colourful wrap-skirts and matching tops in bright blues, yellows, greens and reds. Others wore traditional African, matching headpieces which made the outfits all the more attractive. Looking across at these elegantly dressed ladies with heads held high and shoulders upright, I thought about Canadians. I thought about myself and what I'd become after twenty years, how, outside of the office, I loved to dress casually and slouch around. My African sisters took pride in their appearances; they looked regal. A few Muslim men wore long flowing robes, a little less colourful than the ladies, but decorated with rich embroidery. They wore little matching hats, perched on their heads. They also looked confident and proud. A few of the people wore casual western-style clothes.

As I surveyed the crowd, I noticed an unusual-looking man among them. He was about 5 feet, 7 inches tall, medium build, and dressed in light beige trousers, a brown pinstripe double-breasted jacket with coordinating beige shoes, a crisp white shirt and a beige tie punctuated with little pink dots completed his ensemble. He was clean-shaven with a neat, short haircut and wore a pair of black horn rimmed glasses which seemed too big for his face. I estimated him to be about fifty years old. Every time I looked across at him and our eyes met, he looked away. I decided to play the same game with him. Every time he looked my way, I looked away. I tried to guess what kind of person he was and concluded he was a businessman.

After a while, I decided to ignore the stranger and tried to focus my attention on one of the ladies in the crowd. I was sitting at the airport ready to embark on the second leg of my first African vacation. I still sizzled from the excitement of the eight wonderful days I'd just spent in Ghana. They'll remain indelible in my mind forever.

Focus needed to be given to my new destination. The dreadful reports I'd received about Nigeria both at home in Toronto and in Ghana was disconcerting. It was well known that Nigeria had been subject to a few coups d'etat, chiefly military, over the years, and the rest of the business world regarded that country as unstable. The current government was a military regime with General Sani Abacha as Head of State. I'd heard that corruption was rampant that one could get absolutely nothing done by government officials, until you greased their palms first. I turned over in my mind the question several friends and clients had asked me in Toronto. "Why on earth would you choose to go to Africa?" Now I asked myself, why on earth am I going to Nigeria?

I began to worry as I thought more about my travel plans to Lagos. Known as Africa's most populous country, Nigeria has a population of about one hundred and twenty million people, four times that of Canada. Nearly a million and a half live in its largest city, Lagos. I knew I could easily disappear there without a trace if I wasn't careful. My plans included spending a week in Lagos on my own then joining Joyce, my sister-in-law, and her family in Owerri, in the southeast. Fear crouched in every crevice of my mind, ready to spring forward and alarm me at the slightest encouragement. Anxiety built up causing my stomach to churn. The joys of my anticipated plan began to dissipate. After surveying the passengers around me carefully, I decided to make friends with a plump black lady with a huge straw basket under her seat. I suspected she was a higgler taking goods back to Lagos to sell for a profit. She seemed like the motherly, friendly type. I thought if she took me under her wing, the trepidation I felt would go away, and I would feel safe. Besides, I was sure she could throw a good punch if the need arose. Measured against her, my five feet three inches, fluctuating size twelve figure, made us look like Mutt and Jeff. As I struggled to put my thoughts together to approach her, Adamson burst into the waiting area, charging through the crowd like the eye of a hurricane.

"I travel one hundred miles a hour to come to say goodbye to yuh as I promise," he said, with barely enough breath to shape the words. He looked like a madman, anxiety was written all over his face.

"I'm so glad you made it." I knew my face had lit up like a Christmas tree.

"I warned yuh dat yuh would be lucky if de flight left before 8:00 p.m.," he continued in his delicious African accent I had grown to love.

"Looks like you are right Adamson. It's 6:30 p.m., an hour after we should have taken off, and I haven't heard a flight announcement yet."

"Come wid me. I don't want yuh to wait on dis flight. Switch to Ghana Airways."

I didn't argue with Adamson. I'd gotten accustomed to doing his bidding. During the past eight days, I'd spent almost every waking moment with him. I'd become fast friends with this tall native

Ghanaian, and had come to know him, and to trust him. He practically dragged me to the Ghana Airways ticket counter, and with the help of one of his buddies behind the counter, arranged the switch. I noticed one interesting thing; Adamson had buddies or acquaintances in all the strategic places. This airport was no exception.

Once my ticket was exchanged, and I was set to fly with Ghana Airways, we went upstairs to the airport lounge. I sat quietly, absorbed in thought, while I sipped my last Ghanaian rum and coke. Adamson drank his usual non-alcoholic malt. What could I say to this dear man? He'd been my companion, tour guide, driver, doctor ... Now we must say goodbye perhaps forever. It was Shakespeare who said, "Parting is such sweet sorrow." He obviously knew what goodbye was all about. I would travel on to Lagos and finally back to Canada, maybe never to see him again. Sitting, looking at Adamson, I wished that moment would never come.

"Yvonne, don't forget me now," he pleaded. "Make sure yuh write me. I will be waiting every day for yuh letter."

He was so special and unspoiled. I wanted him never to change. Adamson looked into my eyes, searching—I couldn't stand it, I looked away.

"You don't have to worry, Adamson; I won't forget you that easily. I'll write when I get home. I don't think you'll hear from me while I'm in Nigeria though, okay?"

"Dat's okay, but one day I will see you in Canada," he said with wistful conviction. A smile formed around my mouth. He was always so optimistic. I felt it would be better not to communicate with him from Nigeria. I didn't want to leave him with a false sense that I had to hear from him. I also didn't want to incur unreasonable expenses for my sister-in-law, besides I knew that the phones worked infrequently there. I suspected I would be kept busy, and wouldn't find time to call or write.

Before the flight's departure was announced, Adamson got up to leave. He apologized for not staying with me until the time to go, but he had prior arrangements to pick up some passengers. I rose slowly from our table. Adamson towered over me as we looked at each other. Watching him standing there, lank, lean and lofty, I thought, no, this can't be goodbye. I raised my face to receive a kiss but instead he stretched out his hand and shook mine.

"We don't kiss in public," he said in a stern yet reserved voice. I could hardly believe this was the man who had pleaded with me a minute before, not to forget him. I wanted to say, forget tradition, forget religion, forget whatever, but I remained silent, telling myself, I must respect his culture. Holding back tears, I felt my two front teeth sink into the soft flesh of my lower lip. With the taste of salty blood on my lips, I watched Adamson's graceful, slim figure leave the airport, and my heart went out to him.

"Did you know that the Nigerian Airways flight is cancelled?" A voice jolted me out of my thoughts. The man in the beige and brown suit, who had played peek-a-boo with me earlier, stood before me. He looked into my eyes and I felt as naked as a new unwrapped bar of soap, as if his eyes penetrated my soul. I wanted to say, go away, leave me alone, I want to think—instead, I pulled myself together instantly.

"I didn't know that; thanks for telling me. I just changed my flight to Ghana Airways anyway," I replied.

"I'm booked on the same flight."

I took a closer look at him. I detected a Nigerian accent

"Are you Nigerian?"

"Yes, I'm Nigerian," he said it with such pride, I looked at him more closely. There was something peculiar about this man. He was not forward or rude. He had a mild humble, almost mystic way about him, and at least, he tried to be friendly by telling me about the flight. I decided at once to forget about befriending the buxom woman with the large straw basket, and instead make friends with this man.

"You're just the person I need to speak with," I said, anxiety in my voice.

"Why do you want to speak to me?"

"I'm going to your country for the first time. I don't know anyone in Lagos and I hear it can be very dangerous. Can you recommend a good hotel for me to stay? By the way my name is Yvonne Blackwood," I extending my right hand. He shook it with a firm grasp.

"You can call me, Suobite. You won't be able to pronounce my first name, it's too long." He gazed into my eyes again, and smiled. I felt as if a black storm cloud suddenly lifted from above my head. Anxieties and concerns I'd felt before, evaporated into oblivion with that one smile from the stranger.

When the flight was announced and we boarded the plane, our

assigned seats were several rows apart. The flight wasn't full however, and there were several empty seats including the one beside me. Just before takeoff, Suobite gathered up his jacket and carry-on-luggage, and joined me. We sat together during the forty-five minute flight from Accra to Lagos and talked about the weather, politics, any topic that came to mind. When the flight attendant handed out the small three-part declaration forms for all visitors to Nigeria to complete, he helped me complete mine. When he read my occupation, he said,

"So you are a banker? I've never met a banker-tourist here before."

"Yes, I've been a banker for many years." I didn't want to talk about myself, and worse, the last thing I wanted to talk about was banking: enough of that impervious corporate milieu and the rat race that one can never win, enough about meeting targets, setting stretch goals, increasing portfolios; enough about attracting, growth, and retention. As far as I was concerned, I'd mothballed my business suits, briefcase and high heels for at least twenty-one days. The task of being informal, inspired and inconspicuous was now my forte. Banking belonged to another world, another place. This is Africa, and we were on our way to Nigeria. I turned the tables.

"What about you? What do you do?"

"I'll tell you when we get to Lagos."

I thought that a strange answer to a normal social question and looked at him from the corner of my eye as we sat side by side on the mid-size 927 aeroplane. He seemed so open and friendly before. Why the mystery about his occupation now? I was becoming intrigued with him. My fears about Lagos had eased, now the terrible stories about that city began to swim around in my head again. I'd heard how adroit the con-artists were, and how they played upon your emotions to get you to believe anything they said. Could this meticulous well-mannered man be a drug dealer, con man or maybe someone from the secret service? I looked at him again, and felt sure he couldn't be any of those things. Although his clothes were neat and coordinated, they were too cheap for him to be a drug dealer. A con man? Well he hadn't tried to con anything from me, and from my observance of him at the airport, he hadn't tried it with anyone else. In fact, I didn't see him speak to anyone during the three hours, we sat in the waiting area. A secret service man? No, he was not inquisitive enough for that. Warm comfortable feelings returned, and I decided to wait for him to tell me more about himself, in his own time.

"Where do you live in Nigeria?" I asked

"Port Harcourt."

"Port Harcourt?"

"Yes, in fact I was born and raised there. I've never lived anywhere else."

"You will not believe this. That is the place, my sister-in-law, told me to go, and she will meet me there." I was ecstatic. I would have company until I was safely with Joyce and her family.

At the Murtala Muhammed International Airport, Suobite and I joined the long immigration queue. While we waited, I tried to formulate the response I would give the immigration officer if he quizzed me about my visitor's visa which Mr. Quainoo helped me acquire in Ghana. He had advised me to have $40 or $50 American currency readily available to "tip" the officer if he tried to be difficult. I felt nervous about doing anything of the sort. I'd never bribed anyone in my life, and I didn't want to start now. Besides, I'd done nothing wrong or illegal to obtain the visa. While I deliberated with my thoughts, I saw a handsome, medium built immigration officer walk from behind the counter. He was dressed in a smart khaki suit with polished brass buttons and black shoes as shiny as a new silver dollar. He headed directly toward us. My heart began to pound like a Congo drum. My palms became clammy. I thought my eardrums were about to shatter; they roared so loudly. What could he want with me? How did he know? I was ready to shout "I'm not guilty!" but the words stuck in my throat. When the officer reached where we stood, he stretched out his arms and warmly greeted Suobite.

"Good to see you, brother," the officer said as they patted each other on the back.

"Good to see you, too; you look well. How are you?" Suobite asked.

"Come with me brother, and I'll process you quickly."

"Sam, this lady is with me. Meet Yvonne," Suobite said.

By this time my body temperature began to normalize but my voice remained in an out-of-order mode. I squeezed a thin smile and nodded to Sam. He whisked us through immigration with no questions asked. I breathed freely once more when I realized I didn't have to pay a bribe or fabricate a story.

Sam was a real gentleman. He steered us through customs so smoothly; the customs officer didn't even ask me to open my suitcase. Afterwards, Sam escorted us to the parking area and ordered a reliable taxi. While the cabby attended to our luggage, Sam arranged for some Nigerian currency for me. Before I left the airport, I had a bundle of nairas, exchanged at seventy-seven nairas to one United States dollar. When I slung my handbag over my shoulder, I felt an additional weight. The largest naira bill is fifty. Two hundred United States dollars converted to 308 bills!

I was so happy with how smooth and easy things had gone, I tried to show my appreciation. I called Sam aside.

"Sam, please have a drink on me," I said as I squeezed a United States note into his hand. Sam opened his hand, looked at the note, laughed, then gave me back the money.

"You don't owe me anything, Miss. What I did, I did for my friend." He spoke in a firm crisp voice. "Glad to be of service."

The blood crept slowly up my cheeks, to my temples and into my hairline where the braids suddenly felt like they were squashing my brains. I suffered excruciating embarrassment. If I could've found a hole to bury my head, I would've done so. I didn't want Suobite to know about the incident, for I knew he would be very upset with me. I imagined him thinking, "The nerve of this Canadian tourist, trying to bribe my friend. Do these North American people know that many Africans have scruples?"

I put the money in my skirt pocket quickly, and walked back to the taxi. I wanted to kick myself. I assumed that all Nigerians were on the take. That was the story I'd been told over and over again, that they are all corrupt. In this instance, however, I intended the money to be for appreciation, not a bribe. I thought Sam would've gladly accepted it. I decided I would be more careful next time.

At 11:00 p.m., Suobite and I arrived at the Lasal International Hotel after a short drive from Nigeria's International airport. The hotel was a good-looking white building, four or five stories high, and secured by a high fence.

The receptionist and attendants were businesslike and friendly. In the lobby, I watched Suobite argue with the cabby about the fare he'd charged. In my opinion, the amount seemed fair, for a quick calculation, converted it to only a few United States dollars, but I was not yet conversant with prices in Nigeria. I figured Suobite knew what he was talking about.

At the hotel reception desk, we surveyed the cost of accommodation. I imagined by local standards the prices seemed high, but my mental calculation computed less than forty United States dollars per night. I thought the prices very reasonable. Turning to me, Suobite asked, "Do you want your own room?"

"Yes, I want my own room." I replied emphatically. The question surprised me. What on earth did he mean? Did he expect me to sleep with him, a total stranger, just like that? I knew it! It was too good to be true. All these bloody men are the same. It doesn't matter how they appear to be charming and respectable, they always have only one thing in mind. Women are always sex objects. I cursed myself. How could I have let my guard down and allowed this slick bastard to get so close to me?

I looked Suobite straight in the eye and geared up to give him a piece of my mind. Before opening my mouth, I remembered all the good things he'd done for me to that point. Calm down Yvonne, I told myself. After all, he did accept my decision without an argument. In fact, he'd said nothing. I began to feel terrible about my thoughts, and suggested to the receptionist that she show us both a single, and double rooms. I was relieved when upon inspection, the double room contained only one double bed. In the end, Suobite and I registered for separate single rooms.

A short while later, after freshening up, I entered the small hotel restaurant and found it empty. The tables were all laid with clean white linen table cloths, accentuated by pale pink cloth serviettes, folded like rose petals protruding from the wine glasses. A young waiter about eighteen years old, dressed in a white short sleeve shirt and black pants came to greet me with a wide grin. He pulled out a chair at a table in the centre of the room, and I sat down. We turned our heads to the sound of foot steps on the glossy terrazzo restaurant floor to find Suobite walking to join me. We ordered tea and toast with guava jam when the waiter informed us that the kitchen was closed.

"So tell me, Suobite, what do you do? You said you would tell me about it when we got to Lagos." I asked as soon as the waiter was out of earshot. I'd waited with some curiosity for the answer to this question, when Suobite did not offer the information on the plane the first time I asked.

"I am a minister," he replied succinctly.

I stared at him with my mouth agape. I tried to speak but I couldn't get the words out. After the shock wore off, I thought, no, I didn't hear him correctly. Maybe he is a government minister.

"A church minister?" I asked.

"Yes, I am a missionary in fact. When we met at the airport in Accra, I was returning from a three-week stint of missionary work in Ghana."

I stared at him while thoughts swirled around in my head like a whirlwind. Oh, that explains why Sam greeted him by calling him brother, he meant a church brother. A minister, a man of God. Of all the people to pick me out in a crowded airport at a time when I was worried to distraction about leaving Ghana to travel to Lagos. I'd heard stories about Nigeria, and in particular Lagos, that were so scary even a native would be afraid to go there alone, much less a stranger. Suobite had appeared from nowhere it seemed, struck up a conversation with me, and soon I discovered that not only was he going to Lagos, but also he would continue to Port Harcourt where he lived and the place where I was going. I pondered the many unusual occurrences that had taken place since I planned this African trip. Were they merely coincidences? I'm not superstitious by nature, but I couldn't help thinking that serendipity had a hand in it. This was one more to add to the list. But I kept remembering Suobite's words as we checked into the hotel.

"Do you want your own room?"

My mind drifted back to the time when I lived with my Aunt Marie in the late nineteen sixties in Kingston, Jamaica. Fresh from the urban area where I grew up, I was naive and unexposed to the ways of the world. There was a minister, Tarsus Augustus Brown was his name, and he lived next door to us. I can see him vividly now, tall, stout with a cool black complexion. He must have been in his mid fifties at the time, for his hair was dispersed with sprinkles of gray. He had one of those churches where the service lasted half a day and the people would shout, clap hands and fall into trances. Tarsus always boasted about his conquest when he seduced one of the young women in the church. Aunt Marie, being very religious, and prim and proper, would reprimand him for committing a carnal sin. Tarsus's words, in response to her reprimand, reverberated in my head.

"Do as I say, not as I do."

Looking at this situation, I asked myself, could Suobite be one of these types? Was he one of those ministers who preached the gospel, but didn't live by the rules? Who could forget the media scandal not long ago, with TV Evangelist, Reverend Jimmy Swaggart and the prostitute? He was a man who preached before millions of television viewers, in a most sincere manner, then the scandal broke. I concluded that this wasn't the case. This minister, hadn't made a move on me. He had accepted my decision without any resistance. Why did he ask me that question? Was it a test? Whatever the reason, I had to find the answer.

We spent the next thirty minutes talking about ourselves. He showed me photographs of his beautiful wife and four children, while I showed him pictures of my handsome seventeen-year-old son and twenty seven-year-old daughter. Suobite said it was tough on the family when he travelled on missionary trips, but that was the nature of his work. He'd given his life to Jesus Christ in 1975 after he experienced a supernatural encounter with God in a dream. He was a general overseer of a few churches in Nigeria.

"Yvonne, do you go to church?"

"Yes, I go to church. Not as often as I would like, but I do make it, at least, Easter Sunday and New Year's Sunday." I felt more than a little embarrassed.

It wasn't that I didn't want to go to church. I chose to. I've made many New Year's resolutions to go to church, at least once per month. Somehow, I couldn't tear myself away from my cosy warm bed, to get to church by eleven o'clock on Sundays. I consoled myself that I have a good heart, for religion is entrenched in me, having grown up with God-fearing grandparents. Since being able to put one foot in front of the other, to my late teenage years, I've gone to church every Sunday come rain or shine. I practically knew the Bible by heart. I even sang in the junior choir and participated in church events. I still live by most of the rules.

"If you do nothing else, I encourage you to go to church more often."

"I will," I said, intending to try again.

Suobite removed his oversized eyeglasses and placed them on the dining table. I looked across at him, and it surprised me how handsome he really was. He had a square jaw-line, deep set dark brown eyes, a well-groomed moustache, and small, even, white teeth.

"You look so much younger without your glasses," I said, staring at his transformed features.

"Well, I am forty-one, just five years younger than you, although I thought, you were younger than me. But you said your daughter is twenty-seven? That is impossible!"

"Thanks, that is a lovely compliment. But how would you know how old I am?"

"I saw your date of birth when you filled out the declaration form on the plane." We both laughed. "How do you manage to look so young?"

"I think the youthfulness is in the genes." I said.

When the waiter brought the bill Suobite argued with him about the cost.

Next morning, after we ate breakfast we headed for the airport with the hope of securing an early flight to Port Harcourt. Before we left the hotel, I tried to contact Joyce but unsuccessfully. The hotel's phones weren't working that day. I would call her when I arrived in Port Harcourt.

"Don't say a word when we get to the airport. I will look after everything. Once they know you are a foreigner, they'll harass you." Suobite advised during the short taxi drive.

The airport was the most complicated one I've seen. I thanked Suobite for being there to guide me. Domestic flights within Nigeria operated from a separate section of the airport, away from International flights. It was difficult to imagine it was the same airport I had arrived at the night before. A world onto itself, the domestic flight area was like a marketplace. People hurried back and forth. Higglers carried huge baskets and cardboard boxes on their heads. When the containers were too heavy for their heads, they put them on carts and dragged them around the airport. The overpowering smell of sweat, urine and overripe fruits wafted through the air. I wanted to retch, but I was determined not to embarrass myself. With a titanic effort, I managed to control my fluttering stomach.

It seemed everyone was trying to sell you something. There were touts, as Suobite called them, working amongst the passengers, selling airfares to wherever one wanted to travel within the country. They weren't the same as the ticket agents behind the counter. Following Suobite's instructions, I stood to one side like a mute who was also deaf, while he haggled and argued about the price of the tickets.

"What do you mean the price is twenty-nine hundred nairas? I paid nineteen hundred nairas just three weeks ago." Suobite said to a tout, his voice a tad louder than it normally was. A fifty- three percent increase in three weeks? Wow! I wouldn't dare ask what was the inflation rate in Nigeria. I saw a very serious businesslike side of Suobite. The tout confirmed that the price had increased drastically, and he couldn't do anything about it. Finally Suobite relented, and I handed over a wad of notes for my ticket. He booked us to fly to Port Harcourt by Oriental Airline. I didn't understand why Suobite hadn't bought the tickets from the ticket agents and he never explained it.

I spent the next eight hours in Suobite's company. He stood guard over me like a lion over his prize cub. The strange people at the airport, hagglers, touts, customs people, none came close to me. Suobite took care of my every need.

We waited three hours in the airport for our flight to take off for Port Harcourt, and during that time, I observed some of the Nigerian men and women. I was fascinated by the markings on the faces of several men. Some were very pronounced. It looked as if someone tried to carve whiskers like a cat's in their badly disfigured faces.

I touched Suobite on his arm, "What are those marks on the faces of those men?"

"They're tribal markings that identify their tribe and where they're from. Those men are from the Yoruba tribe from western Nigeria."

Looking at one of the young men, I was overcome with pity.

"My God, did they have to ruin his face for the rest of his life? Couldn't they mark his arm or his chest?" I asked passionately.

"Shh, not so loud." Suobite whispered when he saw the men looking at me.

— ✧ —

I went over and over my encounter with Suobite. He was like a guardian angel. But the nagging question persisted.

"Do you want your own room?"

As if in slow motion, I replayed each scene with him, the things he said, and the things he did. Every time Suobite had to pay money, he argued about the price. Was this just a habit? Or maybe a cultural thing?

While travelling in a taxi toward Suobite's office, the answer came to me in a haze. Cash! Cash was a scarce commodity for him. He wanted us to share a room strictly because of economics! No doubt, this was done often in Nigeria. Again, I scolded myself. I'd focused too heavily on one dimension of the male-female interaction, assuming that this man was after my body.

On the other hand, I quickly forgave myself, for it was an experience I'd lived through time and time again. Most of the black men whom I met were not interested in mere friendships. It was always something with a sexual connotation, and it didn't matter if they were single, married or in between. I'd been conditioned to think that way from past experiences.

With doubts erased and my faith restored, I turned my attention to the beautiful landscape. Our arrival at Port Harcourt gave me the opportunity to take a careful look at Nigeria. Although I'd been in the country for one and a half days, I had barely seen anything as I moved from airport to hotel to airport.

Bordering on the Atlantic ocean, Port Harcourt is in the most southerly part of the country. I gazed at the passing landscape through the open windows of the taxi.

"So this is your town, Suobite." I said, as I watched the luxuriant green trees swaying gently in the wind. Despite the heat, a gentle ocean breeze fanned my face making the temperature bearable.

"Yes, this is my hometown. They call it the garden city. It was here the Westerners made some of their first contact with us."

"That is interesting," I said deep in thought. So this is where it began. I imagined the kind, innocent Africans, welcoming the Westerners, probably believing them to be special people. Little would they know, they were inviting the mongoose into the hen house. "Is the area famous for anything?" I asked, while observing the preponderance of mango trees, alive with blossoms.

"Yes, oil and natural gas. They are the major industries. Most of the major oil companies are here, Mobil, Shell, all of the big ones."

"That explains why it's such a busy city," I offered, while watching the brisk traffic move through the streets.

We alighted from our taxi at Suobite's church office, tired, hungry and thirsty. Hunger disappeared momentarily when three charming ladies and two men rushed to greet us with shouts and laughter. I stood back and watched the spectacle. One would have thought they were kids, and Santa Claus had arrived in town. They were excited and overjoyed to see their leader and friend. They welcomed me again and again as each person looked me over, trying to figure out who I was but, of course, they dared not ask.

Everyone wanted to share stories with Suobite immediately. I'd never seen him smile so much in the one and a half days we spent in each other's company. He was animated, excited, and keen to be brought up to date on the happenings. Without a doubt, this gentleman: minister, missionary, good shepherd, and my guardian angel, was glad to be home.

PORT HARCOURT

*S*uobite didn't abdicate the responsibility he'd voluntarily taken on. He made me comfortable in his small private office, offering a cool drink while he dispensed with church and community business requiring his attention. I glossed over a few small inspirational books he'd published and realized he was a man of great depth. I flipped through a photo album that lay on his cluttered desk, and saw pictures of members of the congregation and his family.

He joined me in the office a short while later.

"Let us pray Yvonne, and thank God for bringing us safely home to Port Harcourt."

We bowed our heads and while he prayed, I said a silent prayer for bringing me safely thus far. After the prayers Suobite looked at me with concern.

"Yvonne, you must be starving." Before I responded, he continued, "I'll get you something to eat."

He commandeered his secretary to take me for lunch.

"Charity, please take sister Blackwood to get some lunch." They had a quiet conversation in dialect, then Charity turned to me.

"Are you ready Sister Blackwood?"

"Sure, where are we going?"

"Not far. Into Port Harcourt."

She was obviously a woman of few words. Suobite made no attempt to leave his office.

"Aren't you coming with us? You must be as hungry as I am," I said.

"It's okay, you go ahead. I'll get a quick snack here." He dismissed us with a wave of his hand.

Charity was a shy, attractive girl of about nineteen. She hailed a cab and we drove a few miles into the bustling town of Port Harcourt. The taxi deposited us at the intersection of a main street and a narrow lane. Charity headed up the lane and I followed closely behind.

Soon we were seated in a large a restaurant. Suobite had assumed I wouldn't enjoy the typical Nigerian foods and had instructed Charity to take me to an English-style restaurant. Several patrons were eating at the tables. A part of the restaurant was uncovered, giving it an outdoor garden effect. Some patrons were dressed in traditional Nigerian clothes while others wore western style suits.

While we sat at the table waiting for a waiter to take our orders, I became aware of the chatter, one of several Nigerian dialects. If only I could understand them. It would be interesting to hear what they talked about over lunch. Were they talking about the stock market? About the approval of a new business loan? Or were they talking about a new government minister?

Before long, a waiter came to our table and Charity ordered pounded yams with chicken soup. I ordered fried chicken and rice, my first real Nigerian meal. It really didn't matter what I ordered at that point, I was too hungry to care. When the meals arrived, we dug in without delay. Although Charity was slim without an ounce of fat on her, she had a mammoth appetite. She devoured the bowl of pounded yams as if it were a small hamburger. I felt inadequate as I daintily ate my rice and chicken. We drank cold refreshing soda pop to wash down our meals, then Charity signalled the waiter for the bill. When the waiter brought the bill, I opened my purse to pay it.

"No, no, no, you don't pay," Charity almost yelled at me.

"It's okay, I have some nairas," I replied, still rummaging through my purse, pleased that Sam had gotten me some Nigerian currency.

"No, Reverend Suobite said I must pay for anything you order."

"Thanks, but really, I don't mind paying."

After seeing Suobite's office and remembering how he argued over every bill he had to pay, I knew he didn't have money to splurge. I took some nairas out of my purse and Charity gave me a searing look.

"Reverend Suobite would be upset, Miss. He told me not to let you pay for anything," she repeated.

I conceded and returned the money to my purse. Why upset everyone? The poor girl would have to account to her boss why I had paid, and the boss would be annoyed. They were only being kind. I had to accept that. She paid the bill and I thanked her for everything. We walked back to the main road, where she hailed a taxi. We sat in the back seat and Charity gave the driver an address. Turning to me, she said, "Reverend Suobite says I must take you to the phone company so you can call your sister."

I'd observed earlier that Suobite had no telephone at his office. The thoughtfulness of this man knows no bounds.

It was eight days since I'd spoken to Joyce from Ghana. During that conversation, I informed her that I expected to get my visa for Nigeria the next day. She had no way of knowing if I'd received the visa, and she didn't know that I was in Nigeria. While the cab sped through the brisk Port Harcourt traffic, I imagined how worried she must be, trying to find out what became of me. I could have kissed Suobite and Charity at that moment. Soon I'd be talking to Joyce! I would assure her I was okay and that I would be with her soon. I could hardly wait.

We arrived at the telephone company and entered a large room with a high ceiling. At one end of the room, two operators sat behind a fenced-in counter. There were several narrow cubicles to the left of the operators, where patrons took their calls once the operators made the connection. Several people sat on the few raggedly chairs which were arranged around the room, obviously waiting to be connected to their parties. A broken-down couch with the stuffing grinning at us like toothpaste spilling out of a tube, was the only seat available. I wrote Joyce's telephone number on a slip of paper and handed it to Charity. She went to the caged counter and handed it to one of the operators, then she joined me on the lumpy couch to await our turn. In between connecting other patrons to their parties, one operator tried unsuccessfully several times to contact Joyce. An hour later, we were still sitting there, waiting. I was no closer to speaking with Joyce than the night I arrived in Nigeria. With much disappointment and anxiety, I left the telephone company. Charity hailed another taxi which took us back to Suobite's office.

I assessed my situation, concluding that I shouldn't impose on Suobite any longer. As the old saying goes, "When men on earth have done their best, Angels in heaven can't do better."

I knew Suobite had done his best. I got up from the chair on the opposite side of his desk, and began to pace the floor.

"Suobite, I think I'd better take my chances and head out for Owerri," I said.

I was annoyed with the telephone system. After so many attempts to connect with Joyce from Toronto, Ghana, and Nigeria, I had hoped for just once, it would work for me.

"Are you sure you want to do that? Your sister-in-law may still be waiting to hear from you. You may have better luck tomorrow." Suobite was very concerned.

"Soon it will be dusk and I don't want to travel unknown roads too late in the night. There's also no guarantee that the phones will work tomorrow. I think this is my best option."

"All right, I'll order a taxi for you. We have a reliable fellow that I use sometimes. I'll get brother Tom to go and get him."

Brother Tom was one of the church brothers who had greeted Suobite when we arrived at his office. When the taxi arrived Suobite instructed Brother Tom to accompany me with the driver. I thanked Suobite profusely for all his kindness. To me he was a true brother, for who would take such pains and such interest to help a total stranger? We'd bonded admirably. During our brief encounter, he'd comforted, fed, protected, and cared for me. I felt indebted to him.

I offered him a donation for his church which he flatly refused. I pleaded with him that it was the least I could do, that it was something I wanted to do. While visiting with him, he'd talked about some of the projects he'd planned for the church. I suggested he use the money toward one of the projects, one of which was to paint the church. Reluctantly, he accepted. I knew the money would be spent wisely, and thanked him for allowing me to participate. He promised to meet with me again before I returned to Canada. I gave him Joyce's full name and university address, and with that we said au revoir.

— ✧ —

Anticipation is probably one of the strongest emotions. It's a feeling of expectation, of awaiting, of hopefulness. It was with this emotion that I set out on the road to Owerri with a driver and Brother Tom. Engulfed in this emotion, I was superhuman, all other feelings took a back seat. I forgot about fear and danger. I was on my way to my sister-in-law, to meet her husband and children, to learn about Nigeria and its culture. A whole new world waited for me to explore.

Suobite had said the trip would take two hours. Two hours was a long time when you're pumped up with anticipation, but I would grin and bear it.

But the two-hour drive lasted three hours. Soon I had my first glimpse of what a military state was about. Every twenty miles or so, we came upon road blockades. Soldiers with long guns drawn, pulled over vehicles randomly to ask questions, and sometimes to search the vehicles. They pulled over our car several times, and each time, when the driver told them I was a tourist from Canada, the soldiers waved us along pleasantly with the popular greeting "You're welcome."

On our last leg of the journey, about ten miles from Owerri, we came upon yet another check point. A group of eight uniformed soldiers manned the post. All carried guns. I assumed the procedure would be like all the others we'd encountered and flashed my pearlies at the soldier who came to our car.

It was at this moment in time that anticipation turned into a nightmare ....

AT LAST, OWERRI

*T*he soldier dressed in fatigues, carrying a long gun, had put the fear of God in me. He'd led me across the street to his boss, citing a charge of illegally importing foreign currency into his country. He had asked what my punishment should be and I presumed the boss would help to make the decision. I was determined to be brave, and not let them see my fear. I quickly wiped the tears from my face with the back of my hand and waited, praying silently. My driver and Brother Tom had followed in silence with the driver still holding up the money taken from my wallet. He could've been a flipping mannequin!

"What's this about?" the boss asked.

"She's importing currency into Nigeria," the soldier said.

The boss looked at the money in my driver's hand, gave a half smile, but said nothing more. He seemed uninterested in my affairs. The soldier continued, looking directly into my eyes. "I think since you're a tourist you should buy me a drink."

I looked at him with disdain. "If it's a drink you wanted why didn't you say so all this time? Here, how much is a drink?" I pulled out a fifty-naira note hurriedly from my purse. "Will this do? Can this buy you a drink?"

I wanted to throw the money in his face, but I restrained myself— he still held a gun. The soldier realizing he was on his own, that none of his colleagues would participate in his game, decided to back off. By now he was too embarrassed to take the money, and I was livid.

"Go on, young lady, I don't want your money, you can go."

I glared at him, and if looks could kill, he would've been stone cold dead. Adrenaline flowed, my blood boiled, I couldn't restrain myself any longer. I decided I wouldn't let him get away with this, and gave him a piece of my mind.

"I've just spent eight days in Ghana, and although they have soldiers on the roads, I never experienced anything like this there.

Everyone was kind and polite. Is this how you treat your tourists? This must be the worst country in the world. I'll tell you one thing, I came here to spend some money but after this, forget it. I won't spend a dime here and I will never come back to this country again!"

I turned on my heels and stalked back to the taxi with driver and escort in tow. I sat quietly in the back of the taxi as we continued our journey, thinking, going over the incident. I looked through the rear window a few times to see if we were being followed, in case the soldier had a change of heart. Thank goodness he never asked to see my passport, therefore, he couldn't know my name. Brother Tom and the driver never said a word about the incident during the rest of the journey.

I decided not to dwell on the incident, instead I tried to relax and willed myself to focus my attention on Joyce. Poor, sweet Joyce must be frantic by now with worry, wondering what had become of me. She would probably blame herself if anything terrible happened to me, chastising herself for encouraging me to come to Nigeria. She must have known about some of the difficulties I would encounter, but she never forewarned me. On the other hand I wanted to console her, to tell her I'm okay, to tell her I take full responsibility for my actions. I wanted so badly to put her mind at ease.

We arrived at the main gate of University of Owerri at 7:00 p.m. There was still some semblance of light, but the sun was disappearing, sliding into the African forest in the west. Two guards were sitting in the small gate-house and one stuck his head out inquiringly.

"Hello there!" I called cheerfully from the opened window.

"Are Dr. and Mrs. Ombede home?" My heartbeat had picked up pace, excitement began to build. I'd made it to Owerri!

"Dr. Ombede, the Vice Chancellor?" the guard asked with a puzzled look.

"Yes Dr. and Mrs. Ombede," I repeated. "Are they home?" He was beginning to annoy me. What's with all these questions, did he not understand English?

"They don't live here on campus Miss. They went home over an hour ago."

"What?" My world began to crumble. I was taken by surprise for this was news to me. "So where do they live?"

Over the years Joyce and I corresponded, but the only address she'd ever given was that of the different universities where she worked. I assumed she lived on campus. When she gave me her card in September, while visiting Canada, the only address printed there was the university address. She never mentioned that she lived elsewhere. At that moment, I wanted to strangle Joyce. How could she forget to give me this important information? Realizing I couldn't commit the crime, I dug deep into the recesses of my mind. How could I, a mature, responsible person, one who advises clients from car salesmen to CEO's, one who others look upon as a role model, how could I overlook such an important detail? As a result of my folly, I was halfway across the globe, in a strange and possibly hostile country, not knowing where I was going. Christ! How pathetic. Shame on you Yvonne Blackwood; you are losing it. Some of your friends were right—you are crazy. Of course, that was the devil speaking. Over the years, I've learned to ignore him. Focus Yvonne, focus. Suddenly, I remembered our plan. Joyce was supposed to meet me at the airport in Port Harcourt. I was to call her upon my arrival there, and she would meet me. It therefore wasn't important for her to give me her home address. She planned to take me home, but we never communicated after I received the Nigerian visa while in Ghana.

"I know the house, but I don't know the address. It is about eight miles from here," one of the gate-men said. Eight miles from the university could be anywhere, east, west, north, south, I needed specifics.

"There must be someone around who can direct us," I said looking around. The university stood smack in the middle of several acres of land, miles away from the main road and far from any settlement.

"No Miss, everyone is gone. We had some trouble on campus."

I was perturbed. I looked at my driver, and the look on his face gave me the distinct feeling he wasn't thrilled with this development. It was obvious that he wanted to return to Port Harcourt. Brother Tom seemed a bit more sympathetic.

We stood outside the university gates deliberating what to do next. Should I return with the driver and escort to Port Harcourt and ask Suobite to put me up? Should I ask the driver to take me to the nearest hotel, and rest up for the night, to return to the campus the next day? Should I ask the driver to take me to a police station to ask for help? After the ordeal, I'd experienced with the soldier earlier that afternoon, I'd lost all faith in Nigeria's law enforcement personnel, besides, with no address, how could the police really help? Maybe I could bunk on the campus grounds until next morning? It was obvious from the tight security, the gatemen wouldn't allow me, an unauthorized person, onto the campus. I was in a dilemma, and I had to find a solution.

While I pondered my options, two cars arrived at the gate and the guard allowed them to enter without questioning them. As the cars drove up the long driveway toward the campus buildings, one gateman remarked;

"That was Dr. Ombede."

"Why didn't you say so before?" I shouted at him. How lackadaisical can these people be? The young men knew I was there to see Dr. Ombede, yet they let him drive right by me onto the campus grounds. Turning to my driver, I yelled,

"Follow that car!"

The driver, Brother Tom and I dived into the taxi before the guard could say, "What are you doing?" and within seconds, we were in hot pursuit of Dr. Ombede's car. We'd almost caught up with his car when it stopped suddenly, and the second car spun around, shielding his car and blocking our path. A beefy security guard in an olive-green uniform, with a black beret perched on one side of his head, jumped out of the first car. With his gun pointed at us, he strode toward the taxi. Before we could figure what was happening, he threw open the door on the passenger's side of our car.

"What are you doing following the V. C.'s car?" he demanded.

He stared unblinkingly at the driver, waiting for a response.

I prayed, "Dear God, please let him ask questions first and shoot later!" I tried to swallow but the dryness hurt my throat. Somehow I managed to get a sound through my vocal cords, a voice that I didn't recognize.

"P-p-please put your gun away, Sir. I'm Mrs. Ombede's sister from Canada. We were trying to catch up with Dr. Ombede. Please tell him it's Yvonne Blackwood in the car."

I tried to keep my voice low and controlled as it returned to normal. I'd had enough guns for one day. The guard returned to the Vice Chancellor's car to deliver the message. In a flash, a slim, medium height man dressed in a dark-blue African robe, came to our car. Assuming he was Dr. Uche Ombede, I sprang from the vehicle with arms outstretched, and gave him the biggest hug I could manage. I forgot about protocol, forgot about tradition, forgot that I'd never met the man before. I didn't care who he was or who was watching us. I was just so thrilled to see him. A surprised look spread across his bespectacled face as he shrank away from me slightly. Not only was he surprised by my sudden appearance, he was also surprised at my sudden outburst of emotions. Two men who were in Dr. Ombede's car and three from the second car converged on us, all curious to know what was happening. After introductions were made all around, I paid the taxi driver and said goodbye to him and Brother Tom. I assured them I was in good hands, and admonished them to relay the information to Suobite as soon as they returned to Port Harcourt.

"Am I glad to see you!" I said, turning to Uche. "I thought you lived on campus. When the guard said you didn't, and he didn't know your address, I was ready to go out of my mind."

"My dear Yvonne, you are a very lucky woman." He spoke slowly measuring each word. He had a calculated intellectual air about him. "Normally, you wouldn't find me here this late, but recently we've had some student unrest. I came back to settle a matter."

How much more luck could I have? I asked myself. With all the problems I'd encountered, from arranging the trip and the relative ease with which they were solved, I had no doubt that someone was watching out for me. How else could I explain the stranger at the airport in Ghana who introduced me to Adamson? And Adamson, who turned out to be an important part of my life for the entire stay in his country? The soft face of Paddy came to my mind, he'd worked behind the scenes although we never met until my final day in Ghana. Then there was Paddy's friend, Mr. Quainoo, who asked for nothing and willingly interrupted his religious fasting period to help me. Without him I would never have made it to Nigeria. Abu came along and helped me feel the real spirit of *Agwaaba*, a feeling of belonging. And the most intriguing of them all, Suobite, my Guardian Angel. How can one rationalize his presence? Yes, someone was making sure I was safe.

Uche made arrangements for his driver to take me directly to his home, promising to see me later that night when he returned. I realized he had important matters to attend to and didn't want to get in his way, besides, now that I knew it would be minutes before I could see Joyce, I was anxious to move on. Later he would learn the full story.

Uche's driver drove skillfully along narrow streets, and in no time we stopped in front of a high metal gate. A pair of eyes peered at us through a small window in the gate, then slowly, as if mechanically, the gate began to open. The driver put the car in gear, and we shot through the opened gate onto the front yard of a huge house. Before the driver could open a wrought iron grill gate which led into the house, five children, four girls and a boy, burst onto the porch and rushed forward.

The children were excited to see me and wanted to inform their mother of my arrival right away. I recognized James immediately, from photographs Joyce had shown me in the fall when she visited Toronto. He headed toward the stairs to tell Joyce the news.

"James, wait, don't say anything. Let's surprise her," I whispered. The children were keen to play the game. They headed up the stairs to their mother's bedroom, while I brought up the rear. At the top of the stairs, the children stayed on the sidelines, out of sight, and I stood dead centre in front of the door while James knocked on it.

"Who is it?" Joyce yelled from behind the closed door.

The quick-witted James responded, "Ma, the Minister of Education is on the phone for you. Can you come down stairs and get it?" Obviously, Joyce didn't have an extension in her bedroom.

"Take a message," Joyce replied. It seemed she didn't hear who was calling.

"Ma, it's the Minister of Education," James repeated with more urgency this time.

"What does the Minister of Education want with me?" Joyce mumbled from behind the door.

"I don't know Ma, but it sounds important."

I heard shuffling behind the door, as if she was trying to put on her slippers or something. Shortly after, Joyce shoved the bedroom door wide open and stormed into the spacious hallway.

The first person she saw was me. She stopped dead, in her tracks. I watched as expressions on her face passed through a spectrum of changes like the colours of a rainbow. I would've paid money to have captured it on camera. It began with disbelief. She wiped her right index finger across her right eye in an effort to clear her vision, but that didn't work. Her expression changed to surprise, joy, relief then disbelief again. A spat of nervous laughter escaped her parted lips and she rushed toward me with outstretched arms. We both laughed as we hugged each other for what seemed like a life time.

"My God, you made it safely. I can't believe you are here, here in my home," Joyce said after she'd grasped the full impact of my appearance. Her voice overflowed with emotions. I too, was overwhelmed.

"Yes Joyce, I made it, and in one piece."

At that moment I couldn't think of anything else to say. A mother can relate to the feelings that flowed through my body. Like carrying a baby full term, then taking maternity leave two weeks before the due date, you wait and wait for D-day. Then one day, when you've almost given up, the child is finally born. Oh, the joy and relief you feel after months of waiting. You want to laugh and cry and sing and shout. I had finally delivered!

We would have several days to talk about my ordeals and experiences. For the moment, we just wanted to let our emotions return to an even keel. The children grinned from ear to ear, oblivious of the ordeal I'd experienced. James had the look of a peacock on his face which said, "I fooled you, Mom."

Later that night, when Uche returned home, he gave us details about the unrest. Students had burnt down the Vice-Chancellor's Lodge at the University in Nsukha. Apparently students from outside were trying to infiltrate Uche's university to stir up trouble. But Uche was well loved and respected by all, and insiders had warned him of the plot which allowed him to quell it before it started. It was for that reason he'd returned to the campus that night. The unrest was brought about by government's imposition of increased fees for university students. Until that time, fees for a university education were minimal. The students were refusing to pay the increase.

Joyce wasted no time, and helped me to settle in and learn the workings of the household. With my self-imposed mandate to check on her well-being and that of the children, I closely observed the actions, attitudes and personalities of the household.

Ada, the first daughter, played mother to her youngest sister. She was eighteen and mature in mind and body. She referred to her older brother as senior brother whenever she talked about him.

James was the dreamer who loved North American designer clothes. He was six feet tall, athletic and obviously missed his older brother who was studying abroad.

Chioma was an attractive teenager who spent most of her time reading in her room.

The noisiest of the children, Nkachiyere loved to play the stereo and hang out with James.

Zelda, eight and the youngest, was very intelligent for her age and loved to spend time with me.

The house was a cavernous white, two-storey building with eleven bedrooms, several bathrooms and two sitting rooms. It was surrounded by a seven-foot-high wall with a gate house, manned by guards twenty-four hours a day. There was always a driver and at least, one car available to take Joyce, Uche, or the children wherever they wanted to go. The garden at the front of the house was framed neatly with small green and white painted stones, but contained no flowers. Greenery was provided by two clumps of shrubs at the right. A few feet from the main entrance a slender tree, with sprawling branches, like the tentacles of an octopus, blossomed profusely. The tree had thousands of tiny violet-blue blossoms, and many fell beneath it to form a beautiful indigo carpet. An exotic aroma from the blossoms filtered through the air intermittently when the wind blew. There was no defined driveway. The front yard was covered with fine gravel which made a crunching noise when you walked on it or when a car drove over it. A black wrought iron grill enclosed the small front porch. If an uninvited stranger escaped the gateman for any reason, his entrance to the house was barred by the wrought iron gate.

The kitchen and household staff operated on two shifts, one set for mornings and another for afternoons. Everyone seemed pleasant and friendly, and they all greeted me with, "You're welcome." I found the use of this expression odd, since Canadians usually say, "You're welcome," in response to someone thanking you first. Later, I found that it was a standard greeting from servants and intellectuals alike.

— ✧ —

My intention was not to spy or carry news, but to merely give assurances to my mother-in-law. A full report would be given to her on my return to Canada. I kept a keen look out for lizards which was one of her great concerns. Based on my experiences in Ghana, I was sure as night follows day, lizards would find me!

I didn't have to wait long. On my second day in Owerri, Joyce and I were standing in the yard waiting for one of the drivers to return after taking Zelda to school. While we stood on the gravelled walkway, a huge lizard, at least I thought it was huge, crawled slowly along the path as if it owned the property. Oh no, not again, I thought. I'd barely gotten over my lizard encounters in Ghana, now I must face another. It had an orange coloured head and tail, while the remainder of its body was a dark hue, a cross between black and navy blue. I held my breath and tugged at Joyce's arm while clenching my teeth, and without moving my lips, while rolling my eyes, I mumbled,

"Joyce, there's a huge lizard coming at us!"

Joyce looked over at me, and realizing I was about to hyperventilate, swung her arms at the lizard and shouted, "Shoo!" The lizard darted into nearby grass as if being chased by a deadly prey.

"You don't have to worry about the lizards here. They're quite harmless."

"Joyce, I can't believe this is you. Your mother is sitting up in Canada worrying to death about you, and how scared you are of lizards, and you're so cool."

"I learned one thing shortly after I came to Nigeria, as you move toward the lizards, they move away, so I don't worry about them anymore, but at first I was scared of them," Joyce said.

I made a mental note. Joyce's mother will be happy to hear that her daughter isn't concerned about lizards. During my stay in Nigeria, I saw at least three other species, but I didn't have to worry about them. They scampered away when I moved towards them.

In the days following, Joyce and I established a routine. Uche, Joyce and I would have dinner together in the dining room after they returned from work. The children ate earlier when they arrived from school. After that, Joyce and I would go visiting, that is, when she wasn't entertaining. Joyce was keen for me to meet most of her West Indian friends and colleagues in the area, I think I eventually met them all.

Owerri is a large city, the capital of Imo State. The main streets were lined with two and three storey buildings containing stores, small shops and offices. Every square had a traditional British-styled roundabout, and there was always a statue of something or someone in the centre.

While driving with Joyce, on one of the many trips I took through the town, I saw a large two-storey burnt-out building.

"What happened there?" I asked, pointing to the building. "Did they have a big fire here?"

"It's a remnant of the Biafran War," Joyce replied.

"The Biafran War? What does that have to do with this place?" I was baffled at Joyce's answer.

"Imo State was a large part of the old Republic of Biafra, also some of the places you've visited, Onitsha, Nsukha and Port Harcourt. The Igbos are the main tribe of this area. Uche is from that tribe."

I was taken by surprise. I remembered the Biafran War vividly. It was a long war from 1967 to 1970. My mind flashed back to horrible pictures shown on television of starving, half naked, skeletal Biafrans. I recalled the suffering and agony of innocent people. It was claimed that a million people died in that war, mostly from starvation. I could scarcely believe that I was actually at the place. Joyce must have realized how stunned I was for she went on to explain.

"After the war ended, they moved some of the state lines and changed the name of the country. Biafra no longer exists." She said that during the war, all bank accounts were seized.

"After the war ended, a new currency was declared and survivors were given a maximum of five pounds. That was to those who were the richest; the poorer ones received less or nothing." These Igbos must be very resilient, I thought. The area didn't seem to be all that badly off.

— ◇ —

One evening, we visited Janice Jamedan. Similar to Joyce, she is a Jamaican who married a Nigerian. She migrated to Nigeria soon after her wedding and has lived there for thirty years.

"I'm so happy to see you Joyce, I'm here all alone except for my servant."

I looked around the large spacious house with all the trimmings of wealthy upper-class family.

"Where is your husband?" Joyce asked.

"Gone on one of the usual medical conventions."

"He's a doctor, and Janice is a nurse," Joyce explained.

Janice, weak and lethargic, curled up in a plush couch in her living room. "I'm suffering from an attack of malaria," she said.

I was appalled. "What's with this malaria business?" I asked. "I noticed some people had it in Ghana while I was there."

"Malaria is always around in these countries. I hope you got your shots before you left Canada?" Janice peered at me inquiringly.

"No, I didn't. I heard the disease wasn't around, so I didn't bother."

"Take my advice, start taking Deaprim tonight."

With her being a nurse and her husband a medical doctor, I was sure she knew a lot more than I did about malaria. She gave me a packet of tiny white pills.

"Take one tonight and one the same day every week for the next four weeks, even after you return home."

I thanked Janice for the pills and her advice. I felt relieved, convinced that I would be safe from contracting the disease. Thank God, I didn't.

The conversation shifted to Kathleen, another West Indian who married a Nigerian in England. On her first trip to Nigeria with her new husband, Kathleen learned the sad, crushing truth. Her husband had four other wives. She loved him dearly and decided to accept the situation and remain with him. She lived in Nigeria for thirty-two years. Her husband died recently. Janice explained what she saw when she visited Kathleen to pay her respects.

"My dear, poor Kathleen sat in a corner of the big living room all by herself. The other wives had their relatives coming and going, comforting them, but not a soul spoke to Kathleen."

"I feel so sorry for her. I wish I could have visited her, but she lives so far from everyone."

"It's occasions like these that show us we must stick together," Janice said with such conviction, I looked at her with keen interest.

"But what can wives such as yourselves do?"

"We formed an organization some years ago called The Niger Wives. At first, it was a social club, but now we advocate and have gotten some changes implemented."

"Are these real changes?" I asked.

"Well, one important example: there was a time when foreign wives like us had to renew our visas every year although we're married to Nigerians and our children are born here. It didn't matter how long you lived here. Now we only have to do this every ten years."

I made a mental note about one man having several wives. It was no myth, it was alive and well in Nigeria. I would garner more information about it from Ada, Joyce's oldest daughter. Later, during my stay in Nigeria, I met people who were first and second wives. Not wanting to appear inquisitive or ignorant, I refrained from asking too many questions.

— ◇ —

Suppertime is a tranquil affair in the Ombede's household, and I always look forward to those times when I had both Joyce and Uche together. We were having supper and the evening servant, a short middle age woman, served a meal of pounded yams with a spicy chicken soup, green salad, topped off with fresh, homemade fruit salad for desert.

"Yvonne, I have a surprise for you," Joyce said as she spooned fruit salad into her mouth. "We're going to visit someone, but I won't tell you who it is. The person doesn't know I'm bringing you over, either."

I looked at Joyce questioningly, but I could see from her toothy grin and the twinkle in her eyes, she wasn't going to divulge any more information. I put my spoon down and looked across at Uche, who had sat quietly during dinner. He looked back and smiled.

"Don't ask me what my wife's up to, my dear, she doesn't tell me everything." He winked at her.

He always referred to Joyce as "my wife." It sounded so impersonal to me, but I could tell he was very much in love with "his wife." Although slim and medium height, Joyce towered about three inches over him, even in flat shoes. He had thick pink lips and always wore pink-tinted eyeglasses.

I was curious about this person we were to visit. Who could it be? I knew no one else in Nigeria which made me very thoughtful. I hope Joyce is not trying to match me up with some man. I'd hate to burst her cupid-like bubble if that was the case but she seemed so pleased with herself. Then again, Joyce is not the type of person to impose her will on anyone. I decided to await my fate. My mind wandered to Adamson's handsome face. What was he doing at that moment? Was he thinking about me? Was he wishing and hoping I'd call? The temptation to call him at that moment, was strong but so was my willpower.

After supper, Joyce ordered one of the drivers to have a car ready. It was dark as we travelled a few miles with Joyce directing the driver, until we ended on a quiet residential street. The houses, all lit up, looked modest but were surrounded with high fences which seemed to be the norm in Nigeria. Joyce told the driver to stop at the house at the end of the street. The driver knocked several times on the gate before a young man opened it and let us in then ushered us into the living room. A medium built, middle-aged man with large dark eyes came forward to greet us. His white shirt was neatly tucked into black slacks. My first thoughts were, this guy is too neat and tidy. He greeted Joyce enthusiastically, showing that they knew each other very well, then he turned his attention to me.

"You must be Yvonne. I pictured you exactly as you are from speaking to you on the phone."

I recognized his voice immediately. "Father Davis! It is you!" I said and rushed to give him a big hug. He was the priest I'd spoken with by telephone in Toronto on New Year's Eve. It was wonderful to finally meet him. I could see it was a pleasure for him, too.

"So you made it to Nigeria after all," Father Davis said, after he recovered from the surprise of my greeting.

"Yes, I made it. It's a long story, and I won't bore you with it. I'm finally here," I said looking around his neat, modest home.

"Well, welcome," he said simply.

"Too bad, I wasn't able to travel with you on New Year's Eve, but that's life. It's so good to meet you."

He offered us hospitality which included *afufa*: a small, green fruit, similar to a garden egg, and a kola nut. By now, I knew the tradition, for Joyce always offered a similar hospitality to visitors at her home.

While visiting Kumasi, I first tried the kola nut. Adamson had bought a few from a street vendor and encouraged me to try it. He was so excited about it that I thought for sure it must be good. I took the small yellow-green fruit from him and sank my teeth into it. When the juice hit my taste buds, my body went into shock! I spat it out so fast, poor Adamson stood looking at me as if I'd grown two heads. It was one of the most bitter things I'd ever tasted. The term "bitter as gall" came to mind.

Now, sitting in Father Davis's house, accepting his hospitality, there was no way I could spit out the kola nut. I chewed it slowly, trying not to grimace as I swallowed the bitter juice. Thank goodness, it was a small fruit. Eventually, I drank pop to get rid of the taste. So much for tradition, I thought.

Joyce had explained some African traditions to me shortly after my arrival, one being, that the kola nut was broken and offered to show unity and brotherly love.

"Until some form of kola is served, a visitor is not fully welcomed," she said.

"Is this done all across Nigeria?" I asked.

"No, this is mainly a tradition of eastern Nigeria, the Igbos." She told me about several other traditions surrounding the kola nut.

"In some areas, the oldest man at a gathering, and in others, the youngest, must break the kola. It must be presented by a son of the soil, a native of the place. At local gatherings, each person, upon presentation, salutes the gathering. The son of the soil prays over the kola wishing all those who share in it, peace, progress and their heart's desire. The prayer must be in a native language for the kola does not hear English."

I was tempted to laugh at that. Does the kola nut hear?

Father Davis was everything a priest should be. He was pleasant, humble and soft spoken. We talked about religion and other topical issues of which he was very knowledgable. Our visit was all too short and I departed from his home feeling the better for having met him.

I was relaxing in the rear living room, curled up like a contented cat, in a brown overstuffed love seat, reading. This room was my favourite, close to the kitchen where the servants brought me cool drinks and snacks before I had an opportunity to ask. It was also away from the children's rooms, a beehive of chatting and laughing. A television and a stereo was stacked in a wall unit along with several books. I could watch television, listen to music, or read. Most times I opted to read.

Joyce called from the main door as she entered. "Yvonne! I have a visitor for you."

She was an hour earlier than usual. There were always visitors at the house, an ongoing stream. I met several chiefs and their wives, university faculty members, people from Uche's village and many more. I wondered how Joyce and Uche kept up with the constant entertaining. I thought this visitor was probable another chief. There were chiefs of varying degrees, tribal chiefs who had constituencies, and chiefs who were given that title because they'd done something outstanding for their tribe.

I smoothed out my skirt with my hands, slipped on my sandals and went to the main living room at the front of the house. I broke into a big grin when I saw who was standing there and hurried over to greet him. Suobite stood there with a big smile.

"Reverend Suobite, my guardian angel!" I said, "how nice to see you again." I held out my arms and we hugged each other.

"Hello, Yvonne." He stepped back to look more closely at me, "You look very relaxed. Are you enjoying your vacation?"

"Oh yes, yes, I'm having a wonderful time. But how did you two connect?" I asked, looking at him, then Joyce.

"Well, after you told me about your sister-in-law, remember you gave me her name and the university where she worked, I went to the campus today and introduced myself. She suggested I come home with her to see you." It was refreshing to hear his rhythmic Nigerian voice once more.

Joyce was obviously pleased to bring him into her home, and invited him to stay and have dinner with us. I was thrilled that we could reciprocate in a small way for all the kindness he'd shown me. We were excited to know more about him while he was keen to make Joyce's acquaintance. He explained that knowing her, would greatly assist him later to help place some of the students of his church in a university.

Between mouthfuls of steamed fish and boiled yams, we chatted amicably all during dinner. We heard more about his strong religious beliefs, his church, his family and his life. By the time we said goodbye, we felt as if he was an old friend. I experienced a deep, warm feeling that I would meet Suobite again, perhaps in the near future.

*T*he journey to Jos came nowhere close to any comfortable car ride I'd previously experienced. Joyce had scheduled a trip that would take me through a cross-section of Nigeria, as I would travel from Owerri in the south central, to Jos in the northeast. I was excited about the trip. Seeing some of the northern territories would give me an appreciation for other parts of the country and help me learn more about Nigeria. Ada and Zelda, Joyce's eighteen- and eight-year-old daughters would accompany me, and Richard, one of Joyce's chauffeurs, would drive.

Jos is the capital of Plateau State, one of Nigeria's thirty-six states at that time. There is no guarantee that this number will hold firm in the years to come for it seems that the number of states and their boundaries change whenever the government changes. Geology of the area shows it is made up of crystalline rock of the Pre-Cambrian age. Famous for the minerals mined there, Jos's major industries include tin, fuel and columbite.

Wednesday morning, the weather was balmy at that time of day as the four of us set out on our journey to Jos. I sat in the front of the mid-size Peugeot with Richard, while Ada and Zelda sat in the back. Soon the sun begun to warm the air, and I knew it would be a hot day before long, hot as all the days had been since I arrived in Nigeria. The days cloned each other. Except for the rising of the sun and the mysterious appearance of the spotlight moon, one could hardly tell one day from the other.

For nine hours, I sat on my derriere as we meandered along dusty roads, climbed steep hills, descended through valleys, careened around blind corners, and crossed murky rivers. Small waterfalls cascaded down jagged mountainsides, their crystal clear water inviting us to stop the car and run through them. Temptation was great for the car's airconditioning was no match for the intense heat. I salivated over the feeling of pure spring water spilling over my sweaty body. It was only inaccessibility from the sheer precipitous hills and tangled mass of vines, and dodders intertwined into heavy underbrush, that held me back, for many of the waterfalls disappeared into the bushes. In contrast, brown abandoned sandy beds of rivers that had dried up, or simply changed courses because of the dry season, stood bare against the forest greenery in some areas.

Richard negotiated pot holes the size of craters. On Nigerian roads, you drive on the left, but on several occasions Richard drove intentionally on the right, just to avoid the pot holes. Sometimes drivers travelling the opposite direction did a similar thing and many times I closed my eyes and whispered a prayer, conceding that we were done for, when Richard and the other driver seemed destined to hit, but through the mercy of the good Lord, he managed to circumvent collisions.

If someone deserved an Olympic gold medal for driving on impossible roads, Richard had my vote one hundred percent. A well-built six-footer, he was pleasant and helpful, but a man of few words.

We travelled through the states of Abia, Ebonyi, Benue and Nassarawa. Every few miles we came upon toll booths stretched across the roads. The toll was five nairas, and once Richard paid it, we were free to continue our journey. Looking at the terrible condition of the roads, I wondered how the toll was used. Certainly not for road repairs!

Up, up into the mesas of Plateau State we climbed, winding around hills, sometimes looking down on the road we had just travelled. The air felt invigorating. I filled my lungs with it every opportunity I had. There is something special about fresh unpolluted air. You breathe it in deeply and immediately your body reacts. You feel light and carefree. I began to experience a feeling of abandonment washing over me.

My memory cells instantly recalled a hike I'd taken into the mountains shortly after graduating from high school. On that unforgettable occasion, a group of six of us from the graduating class took a weekend hike to the Blue Mountain Peak, the highest mountain in Jamaica. As the six of us climbed the steep hill, amidst teasing and jeering from each other, we could see the road we'd just travelled spiralling around the mountain. Unusual birds darted over our heads twittering sweet songs of freedom. Unknown berries, berries we never knew existed, winked at us, daring us to taste and see. The Blue

Mountains towered high above all other mountains at seven thousand four hundred feet above sea level. It seemed we were looking down on the world below. It was rumoured that on a clear day, if one stood atop the metal tripod which was anchored on the peak, one could see Fidel Castro picking his teeth in Cuba! But it was the crisp enchanting air that fascinated me. There was nothing like it.

I had never experienced anything like it until now. Ascending the hills of Plateau State, although not quite as high as the Blue Mountain Peak, the highest point being four thousand three hundred feet, the air felt similar. But alas! My recollections were shattered when the first puff of smoke hit us. I looked through the opened car window, to my right, and saw flames leaping several feet into the air while black smoke curled toward the sky. A large fire blazed scant few yards away from the road on which we travelled. What will we do now? I wondered. Richard drove by without as much as a glance.

"Hey Richard, what's going on over there?" I asked.

"Nutting Miss, dey clearing land to plant someting."

I understood instantly what he meant. My grandparents, their generation, and generations before them, had done a similar thing in Jamaica. They burned trees, grass and shrubs to clear the land, then they ploughed it to prepare for cultivation.

"I see they're using the old-fashioned method of clearing," I remarked, expecting a response from Richard. He ignored me. I saw several other small patches of smoldering fires, and billows of smoke as we drove on.

"Do they ever have any large bush fires because the farmers couldn't put out the flames on time?" I asked.

"I don't know. I neva hear about any." Richard sounded uninterested in the conversation, so I decided to remain silent and take it all in.

While travelling through the valleys, every few miles we came upon similar small fires. The smoke always seemed to blow toward my side of the car. I don't know what it is about smoke, but in Canada, whenever I'm out with friends who smoke, the smoke always, curls toward me, the non-smoker. I was convinced that, by the time we arrived in Jos, we would be reeking of smoke.

— ✧ —

We passed through several towns of varying sizes and in each the market scenes were similar: dozens of vendors lined the streets, selling their wares, from clothing to vegetables, to gates. Never have I visited a country where gates were such popular items.

Gates in Nigeria are by no means ordinary. They are huge metal contraptions of all colours and designs. Some are best described as works of art they're so exquisite. You could purchase a gate with a design of your choice, from a pair of lions to cupids. A gate could be bought at the side of the road privately, from one of the roadside markets, or at one of the permanent markets.

So what do you do with this wonderful gate you ask? I'd observed that all the larger houses were surrounded with high fences or walls. Some fences spanned six feet, or higher. Entrance to these properties had to be via a gate and only after someone from within allowed you to enter. Gates had to be wide enough to allow a car to drive through. Since the gates are already made, you need only to purchase and install them.

As we drove through towns and villages, I wanted to take photographs of some of the fabulous houses, but high fences obscured my view, allowing me to see only snippets of the structures, mainly roof tops.

During my stay in the country, a hot topic of discussion was whether the government should impose limits on the height of fences. It was perceived that wrongdoings were taking place behind some of these high enclosures.

In contrast, while the well-to-do protected their homes with ostentatious gates and high fences, some of the poorer class still lived in mud huts. Several times along the way, we came upon little colonies of mud huts. Having arrived in Africa with preconceived ideas about the poverty of the country, the sight of huts didn't surprise me, for the media had done a good job of projecting them. The surprise was, I saw very few. It suggested to me that living in mud huts was not the norm but the exception, at least, in the areas where I travelled.

Turning to Ada in the back of the car I asked, "Who actually lives in those little mud huts?"

"Just regular people like you and me, and we don't call them huts. It is the white man's derogatory way of speaking. They are mud houses." Ada sounded as if she wanted to get something straight and I got the message.

"Thanks for that information Ada, I wouldn't want to call it the wrong name."

"In all areas people originally lived in mud houses. My father grew up in one of them and many of the rich sophisticated people you've met, grew up in mud houses."

"That is really amazing," I said.

"They remain as a sign that the occupants haven't progressed materially, they could be older folks or they're still illiterate or traditional. But don't worry, you'll be surprised to know that some of the younger ones are getting educated and leaving it behind for the towns." Ada was a bright young lady, waiting to get into the medical program at the main University of Nigeria. I could always rely on her for factual information.

Sometimes the grouping of mud houses consisted of three, but most times they were more than five. The size of the mud houses varied, and they were usually arranged in a circle with one in the centre. The centre hut was usually not fully covered to the ground as the others, so that as we drove by we could see wooden seats inside.

I asked Richard why the centre hut was different, and he explained that the elders held their meetings in it.

"Why are they clustered in groups?"

This time Ada answered, "They cluster to show a collection of related families. It includes related nuclear and extended families. They do that for protection, socialization and identity. It is a collection of these clusters that make up a village."

Some of the houses were neatly contoured, with mud smoothly applied like soft icing on a cake. The roofs were always made of thatch. Miles and miles of tall grass grew along the roads we travelled, and I assumed it was used to make roofs for the mud houses. My only regret was not having an opportunity to go inside one of the mud houses and to get a feeling of how the community worked.

In the towns traffic snarled as drivers tried to avoid hitting pedestrians who were intent on selling their goods with no concern for their safety. The market scenes were always colourful. Vendors dressed in multicoloured Nigerian cotton garments gesticulated to passers-by to purchase their goods. There was nothing unmacho about wearing multicoloured clothing in Nigeria. Men and women wore it. A smile played around my mouth as I remembered my teenage son refusing to wear a fashionable cotton shirt I'd bought for him while on a trip to New York.

"Robert, why don't you like the shirt?" I'd asked, feeling disappointed that I'd wasted hard-earned money.

"Mom, the shirt is pink. I don't want it. Guys don't wear pink."

"But it's pale pink," I said, imploring him to wear it.

"It's still pink," he said with finality and that was that.

I know my son well. He is as stubborn as a coffee stain on a white blouse. I knew he would become more adamant if I tried to force the issue. The pink shirt has a permanent place in my closet. I wear it around the house sometimes. It suites me fine except for the awkward way of buttoning it. Mischievously, I thought of buying my son one of the colourful outfits. It would certainly have sent him ballistic. Eventually, I bought him a vest with a black, back panel and a red, green and yellow pattern on the front. If he didn't like it, he could cover up most of it with a jacket.

I was curious about the wrap shirts worn by most of the female vendors, for they were precariously hitched at one side. I saw no pins or hooks with which they were fastened. I wondered if they ever became undone, falling to the ground, thus revealing the wearer's undergarments. Matching tops and flamboyant headgear always added a splash of colour to the scene. Invariably the outfits were completed with the ever popular push-toe rubber sandals worn by both male and female. I was astounded how Nigerians were able to walk long distances in those thongs. I even saw men riding motor cycles while wearing them. Among the crowd were always people dressed in regular western clothing. Markets were rarely structures of bricks and mortar, but more a series of slightly-built booths and stalls placed along the roads. Vendors were all ages, from young nine year olds to great-grandmothers and grandfathers. Haggling was expected, Richard informed me.

"Yuh neva pay the fust price dey ask," he said.

I understood him perfectly. I could see Adamson animatedly haggling with the vendor in the crafts market in Accra when I bought the carvings. It was simply a way of life, their way of life. For me, from a society always in a hurry, it was an annoying thing. Tell me the best price the first time, and we have a deal. Making me sweat by haggling back and forth is a guarantee that you'll never get my business.

The first time I bought a new car, the salesman tried the haggling thing with me. Shortly after entering the Chrysler dealership, I'd fallen in love with a tan coloured Volare and made an offer to the salesman. He kept going back and forth to his sales manager who never came out of his cubby hole to speak to me. Finally, after the salesman had gone to his boss the third time, I became angry.

"Listen," I said, "when you've made up your mind on what is a good price for the car, you can call me. I'm going over to the GM dealership next door." I began gathering up my purse, calculator and note pad. The sales manger, who'd remained in the background up to that time, sped over to the desk like a fire truck on call. Before I got up to leave, he had the price I'd offered to pay scribbled on his note pad. I detest those games.

Halfway into the journey, we stopped at a roadside market in the town of Benue, where we purchased ripe bananas and peanuts. Ada instructed me from the back seat of the car, how to eat both together. As I sat in the blistering heat, eating bananas and peanuts, Adamson floated into my consciousness. I recalled the night we went dancing in Accra, then stopped at a street vendor to buy fried plantain and peanuts. I closed my eyes and took deep breaths. If only he were here. He would be showing me things and explaining the culture. He would be telling me stories to make me laugh. His deep rhythmic voice echoed in my head. There were no two ways about it, I missed him.

Snapping out of my thoughts, my eyes followed Zelda. She was a delightful little girl with big bright eyes and tiny white teeth. Ada played the role of mother when Joyce was too busy and she'd combed Zelda's hair into a bushy ball, up on top of her head then tied it with a rubberband with two large red beads. Zelda was big for her eight years and extremely intelligent. Joyce dressed her in the cutest little dresses. Today she wore one with flowered patterns of pink and green with streamers at the waist, that were tied to form a big bow at the back. Zelda devoured the ripe bananas like a monkey at dinner time. We teased her, calling her Chimpy the rest of the trip.

Because we travelled on a weekday, we saw hundreds of students moving about on the roads and in school yards. All wore uniforms, each school having its designated colour. The girls looked smart in their tunics of almost every colour of the spectrum, from chocolate brown to red, to purple. The boys wore khaki pants and shirts.

My mind recaptured the nostalgia of my elementary and high school days. In Jamaica, all elementary students wore similar uniforms, mainly navy blue tunics and white or pale-blue blouses. In high school, uniforms were more colourful, each school having its own design and colour. At my high school, Manchester High, the girls wore bright green tunics, black shoes, white socks, and white blouses.

Looking back at those days, I marvelled at the wisdom of the person who made the rule that white socks and white blouses should be worn. The soil in that part of the country was red, rich in iron ore and bauxite. Imagine the challenge to maintain white socks and white blouses in an area where we were constantly bombarded with dust from red soil which blew all year round. But we did it.

The older folks were no academics, many could barely read, but they knew about the sun's powerful ability. In fact, they knew a lot of other things, including the medicinal properties of the herbs and plants around them, and the best time of year to plant certain crops. They taught us how to soak white garments in soapy water, and without removing the moisture, to place the garment in the sun on a flat surface, a sheet of zinc or even a smooth rock. Within an hour or two of exposure to the sun's rays, all traces of the red dirt disappeared. The final touch was to rinse the garment in clean water, coloured with a pinch of blue mixed in. Voila! The white clothes were as white as table salt. Today we use chemicals such as bleach, sometimes to the detriment of the garment.

Then there were the rules: We had to arrive at school on time and our uniforms had to be neatly pressed. A challenge if ever there was one. How many teenagers can travel five, sometimes as many as twenty miles by public transportation, sitting during the journey, and arrive at their destination with clothing uncrushed and every pleat in place? We had a regular routine to beat this challenge. My classmates and I, upon entering the bus, would put our hands behind us, and while the bus rocked to and fro', our hands followed the contours of the vertical pleats in our tunics, reshaping each one carefully. When we were satisfied that all pleats in the derriere section were lined up straight, like little English ladies, we sat down. We never plopped down onto a bus or car seat, and when we arrived on campus our starched tunics were crisp and wrinkle free.

The boys had it a lot easier for they wore generic khaki pants and shirts. On the shoulders, they wore epaulets made with their school colours and crest to differentiate one school from another. It was easier for them to do mischief without being caught, for by removing the epaulets, no one could identify which school they attended.

— ◇ —

We were driving slowly through a town, when I saw a group of a dozen people sitting by the side of the road, a short distance from the markets and the crowds. They wore old, worn clothing that appeared dark brown from accumulated dirt and grime. Huddled together they seemed detached from the rest of the people.

"Who are those people?" I asked. "Are they some kind of a religious sect? Why do they cover their faces?"

"Dey are lepers," Richard replied.

"What?" I wasn't sure I'd heard him correctly.

"Dey are lepers," he repeated.

I was shocked, "You mean those people have leprosy?"

"Yes, they have leprosy." Ada confirmed.

"I thought that disease was eradicated centuries ago."

As soon as I said that I remembered Mother Theresa, winner of the 1996 Nobel Prize. She'd received a lot of media coverage living among lepers in Calcutta, India. It surprised me. I didn't expect to find leprosy in Nigeria in this modern age.

"It is still around," Ada said. "I don't know why they are so near the road. Usually they keep a good distance away."

From the little that I knew about that disease, it has caused immense suffering since biblical days. The Bible story of Christ healing the leper is well known. It is a horrible, disfiguring, contagious disease. How on earth do they control such a thing in Nigeria?

Richard must have sensed my unease for he suddenly sped through the town as if we had a train to catch. I breathed a sigh of relief. It was bad enough thinking about the possibility of contracting malaria, but leprosy? That was too much for my vacation-relaxed brain to grasp.

After several more hours of meandering and obstacle dodging, we entered the outskirts of the capital of Plateau State. Jos was one of the most picturesque places I've seen. To envision this place, you must close your eyes for a moment and cast your mind back to some of the old Western movies. Think of John Wayne lumbering along on his horse through a parched desert, with mesas looming in the distance. Remember those huge boulders jutting out of the ground as he rode by? If you visualized that scene, you've seen parts of Jos. Hollywood could've easily made a Western movie there with minimal stage props.

Richard stopped the car, allowing us to take in our fill of the scenery. Under cloudless, azure skies with the sun pelting down on our hatless heads, we viewed the most magnificent boulders. Rocks were scattered all around or piled high into mounds in some areas. Intermittently, scrub bushes—small trees—managed to grow and remain green despite rocky soil and lack of rainfall. Plateau State lived up to its name. How entirely different this scenery was from Owerri where Joyce lived. It was difficult imagining this was still Nigeria. It was as if we'd journeyed to another country.

Deeper and deeper we drove into the State. In the foreground, craggy mountains gaped at us, while in the distance they looked grey and hazy. I learned later that the haziness was caused by a dust-laden wind, the Harmattan, which blew into Nigeria from the Sahara desert. A brilliant sun shone with the intensity of a desert sun. The mesa-type mountains looked parched and barren. Giant cacti, over ten feet tall, stood like sentinels along the road, green and succulent.

But for me, the most intriguing were the huge boulders. They stood on the hill sides as if placed there by the Gods. Some appeared as if they were on guard, looking down on the feeble humans toiling beneath the mountains. Some appeared like huge birds of prey waiting to pounce on unsuspecting, small animals. While others huddled in groups like a herd of cattle, still others stood alone like brave warriors. The shapes and sizes were incredible. Excitedly, I asked Richard to stop the car again for a photo opportunity. This was a time I wished I had a zoom lens. One particular boulder looked genuinely like a giant bear, I kept expecting it to move!

We clambered out of the car, keen to stretch our limbs and to enjoy the crisp mountain air. Zelda was anxious to pose with her newly-found aunt, and I was happy to grant her the favour, provided we captured some of the intriguing boulders in the background. Amongst the chaos of huge boulders we posed on top of, beside, under and in front of them.

As we came closer to our destination, the brilliant sun became a magnificent red ball of fire. I asked Richard to stop, and once more we exited the car. We climbed a small mound and with our backs against a large boulder, we focused our eyes on the heavens above. Within moments, the sky and all the mountains became illuminated as it were, with a tiny spray of red dust. The mountains had appeared hazy-blue to this point. It seemed as if a magical fairy flew across the sky, and with a mega aerosol can, sprayed the whole area with micro particles of sun dust. The entire mountain range glowed orange-red. We watched from one side of the mountain while the sun sank lower and lower into the western sky on the other side. Not long after, the final rays of the sun faded, the intense heat dissipated, and gentle cool air took its place. After Richard and the two girls returned to the car, I stood looking at the sky in awe, wondering what miracle it was that I'd witnessed. I've observed many sunsets before. Caribbean sunsets can be spectacular and romantic, and have inspired many painters and photographers, but this sunset, this Jos spectacular, was the most dramatic one I'd ever witnessed. It remains indelibly imprinted in my memory.

— ✧ —

Before we left Owerri, Joyce had given me a letter. "When you get to Jos, before you check into a hotel, please stop at the University of Jos and ask for Mabel Ojo, the Registrar. This letter is for her."

"A good friend of yours?" I asked.

"Not quite, I met her last November at a conference, and she was quite a nice lady. She may even put you up."

I took the note and promised to look up Mabel. I always thought Joyce was a person with simple values in spite of her illustrious academic education. Dr. Joyce Ombede indeed! Why would she think a woman she'd met only once, at a conference at that, would put up four total strangers because they stopped by to say hello? I had more than adequate funds to cover hotel and other expenses so paying for accommodation was not a concern. Being the independent person that I am, I certainly wouldn't want to depend on strangers in that way.

We arrived at the University of Jos and stopped at the main gate to inquire about Mabel Ojo. The gates were controlled by two guards in a small gatehouse. All the universities were guarded similarly. When I'd visited the University of Nsukha few days earlier, the guards had checked the trunks of all cars as they left the campus. This was a change from the Universities I'd attended in Toronto, where students and the public had free, easy access to enter and leave the campuses at any time.

While Richard asked the guards at the gate for information, a man of medium height, dressed in a dark pair of slacks and a T-shirt stood nearby listening to the conversation.

"You want to know where the registrar lives?" the stranger butted in before the guards had a chance to answer Richard. I thought the man was rather forward since no one had addressed him.

"Yes, we want to know where she lives. Do you know?" Richard asked.

"Yes. If you turn around here and go back up the road two miles, you'll come to ... tell you what, I'll come with you in the car and show you the way. It's easier, and I was going that direction anyway," the man said.

Richard said something else in dialect and before I could protest, I'd joined Ada and Zelda in the back seat of the car while the stranger took my place in front. He directed us expertly to the registrar's house. A gatekeeper peered through a metal gate and quickly opened it to let us in. He didn't ask us any questions. I thought it strange. What was the point of guarding a gate, if strangers are not questioned before they're allowed to enter?

A sprawling one-story building with a terrace blanketed with dozens of flowerpots containing African violets and ferns stood before us. A vineless trellis covered the walkway to the front door. I figured one of the occupants must have a passion for gardening. It had to take a good chunk of someone's day to water all those plants.

"She is not home, I don't see her car," the stranger said.

He told Richard to park on the grass near the front porch and we joined him under the trellis. He knocked on the front door. There was no response. The strange man retrieved a key from his pocket and threw open the front door.

"Come in, come in, and have a seat," he urged, pointing to the sofas in the living room. At first we hesitated, but assuming he must know the registrar very well to have a key, we followed as directed. It had been a long day and I was too tired to argue. Besides, every bone in my body cried out for help. He yelled something in one of the Nigerian dialects toward the back of the house.

Instantly, two teenage boys came forward.

"Get the guest room ready and heat up some water for these people," he commanded.

The two boys disappeared to the back of the house.

He turned to me, "So what is your name?" We were sitting in the living room. The furnishings were old and simple, but the room generated warmth. It was a homely warmth of love and fellowship.

"Well, my name is Yvonne Blackwood. I'm Joyce Ombede's sister visiting from Canada, and these are her two daughters, Zelda and Ada."

Joyce and I had decided to tell everyone in Nigeria that I was her sister as this saved us a lot of explaining. The first time Joyce introduced me to a Nigerian colleague as her sister-in-law, the woman asked how was my husband. It took some time to explain that I was no longer married to Joyce's brother that I was really her ex-sister-in-law, but we remained friends ... too much explanation. For the rest of the trip I was adopted, I became a sister.

"Richard is our driver," I said, pointing to Richard. "So what is your name? You seem to know your way around here."

"I am Professor Ojo, the registrar's husband!"

Four pairs of eyes focussed on the professor, and we all burst into laughter simultaneously.

"Why didn't you tell us you were Mabel's husband when we asked for her at the university gate?" I asked. "You had me thinking you were a gardener or some such lowly person when we first saw you." Feeling badly about my previous thoughts, I wanted to express greater respect, but there was no need to worry about that. It did not take us long to warm up to the friendly, animated professor.

His skin was smooth and very dark. I couldn't figure out his age, for he had no wrinkles and no noticeable grey hairs. His piercing dark eyes roamed around at all times. If the lights were turned off, and the room was in total darkness, I'm sure I would still see the whites of his eyes. Almost every sentence he spoke was funny. He reminded me of a cuddly teddy bear. By the time Mabel arrived home, an hour later, we were relaxed and comfortable.

Mabel was petite, five-foot, fair-skinned, and just as warm as her husband and she greeted us like family. A native Trinidadian, she married Dr. Ojo, a Nigerian, and had lived in Nigeria for thirty-four years.

Later when I thought we'd socialized enough, I inquired about a hotel for us to stay. They looked noticeably upset. To this couple the idea of us staying in a hotel in Jos, their hometown, was unheard of. They offered the guest room without any request from us. Richard would share with one of the sons, the two boys, whom we saw earlier. Both were attending university. "Prof" as we dubbed Dr. Ojo, expressed his indignation for people who treated drivers, servants and the like, with inferiority. How different from Joyce and Uche, where servants and drivers well knew their places.

In no time, like one big happy family, we were sitting at the dining table eating steamed fish, boiled yams and cooked vegetables which Mabel prepared, while Prof, who was on staff at Jos university, told us local folklore tales.

For a while, we volleyed stories back and forth. Prof told us local proverbs or stories, and I tried to match him by telling Jamaican versions of similar proverbs or stories. We covered a wide variety of topics based on the many Nigerian tribes. Topics covered the disabled/ deformed, heroes, sexuality, gods and a mother's love.

"A youth who sees an elder with deep eyes (a hollow face) should not laugh at him. Instead, he should ask the elder to tell him about his experiences. This one is from the Yoruba tribe," Prof said.

"One day the piglet said to the mother pig, 'Mother, what makes your mouth so long?' The mother pig turned to piglet and said, 'son, don't worry, you're growing up, one day you'll soon find out.'" That was my matching Jamaican proverb.

"One should never laugh at a sick or a deformed person; perhaps what affects him today may affect you tomorrow."

Another Nigerian saying.

"Today fe mi, tomorrow fe yuh," I countered with a Jamaican proverb.

"Deformed persons are also used ritually, and among the Yoruba tribe for example, the man of a wife who continues to produce stillborn babies would be required by a native doctor to have sex with a mad woman. One important instruction is that he should not wipe his organ, but go directly to his wife and have sex with her. After that he will be able to produce children who will not be stillborn."

I didn't have any stories to match that one. In fact, I think my memory bank dried up after that! It was so incredible. Looking around the table, I noticed Zelda's wide eyes and her antenna pointing straight up.

"Zelda, I think it's way past your bedtime," I said.

"Can't I stay up a little longer?" She asked in her pleading innocent voice.

"No. It's very late and we have to wake up early in the morning." Reluctantly, she got up to leave. "Little piggies have long ears," I said, winking at Prof.

Ada followed her to the guest room. Prof had listened to my stories and proverbs attentively, and he asked me to jot down a few for him. It was my pleasure to do so and in return he gave me one of his publications.

That night I slept peacefully. It was the best sleep since arriving in Nigeria. Tiredness from the long trip to Jos was a factor, but the cool night also invited sleep, for Jos was several degrees cooler than the southern parts of Nigeria. I didn't have to rely on airconditioning to keep me cool.

The next morning I awoke to the sound of jangling cutlery, rattling pans and crackling dishes. Prof and Mabel were in the kitchen fixing breakfast. I woke up Ada and Zelda and we joined our hosts for breakfast. During the meal Prof piped up cheerfully,

"I don't have to teach classes today." A likely story, I thought. "I'd love to show you all around Jos."

"You read my mind." I said, beaming appreciatively. "That would be lovely, thanks for offering."

"Take them over to the university," Mabel suggested.

"Yes, we'll do that first." Prof agreed.

"What we'd like to do is, do the tour then leave Jos later this evening and try to reach Benue before dusk. We'll book into a hotel in Benue tonight and return to Owerri tomorrow," I said.

"You should be able to do that, the weather is good," Prof said.

Mabel was not as fortunate as Prof, she had to work. I expressed my appreciation for her kindness by telling her how graciously she'd accepted us into her home and made us welcome without hesitation. We hugged each other when we said goodbye, then she dashed off to work as I felt the tears gather at the corner of my eyes.

Prof took us on a tour of the campus of the university of Jos as Mabel suggested. It seemed everyone knew and loved him, he was greeted warmly by staff and students alike. He made a special effort to introduce us to the Head Mistress of the University Primary school. A charming lady, Thelma Uku was a Trinidadian native. She seemed pleased to meet a fellow West Indian. I regretted not being able to spend more time with her, but Prof was anxious to move on.

Later, we visited the Jos zoo and the pottery museum. The small museum was a fascinating place. Pottery of all shapes and sizes were on display. Some were hundreds of years old. Some African tribes used to bury their dead in huge vase-like pottery. While inspecting the containers, it occurred to me that it must have been a chore to stuff a human body into a vase. Maybe the people from that particular tribe were very short? I felt a spiritual reverence about the place and moved about carefully, ever aware of its history and importance. Zelda and Ada did the same. It was as though the ancestral spirits were watching us.

At the end of the museum tour, we proceeded to a little gift shop in the compound. What happened next did not totally surprise me, but a wide grin always appears when I recollect that day.

My chance meeting with Prof at Jos's university gates was an amusing one, and I must admit that his behaviour was odd. At the gift shop Prof further exhibited his eccentricity. He harassed the poor store clerk to bring out several tribal outfits, which he tried on and paraded before us to inspect. There was laughter all around as the busybody professor dressed and undressed, and modelled the outfits. At one point, he decided to include me in the act and dressed me like a member of the Tiv tribe! Tiv is one of the two hundred and fifty different ethnic groups in Nigeria.

The material was a heavy handwoven black and white stripe. While we were both dressed in the tribal garment, he ordered Ada to take photographs of us. Even the frustrated clerk laughed at his antics. Finally, when he'd exhausted the clerk enough, he left the store without purchasing a single item.

The clerk's disappointed look tugged at my heart strings. I think I saved the day, and put the smile back on his face, for by the time I left the store, I had bought beads, earings, prints, and post cards.

Since my arrival in Nigeria I'd searched high and low for post cards to mail home on which would be written the usual, "Having a wonderful time, wish you were here." I couldn't find a postcard anywhere. I got the impression tourism was of no importance to the country. That may explain why the soldier had harassed me on the road to Owerri. While searching the gift shop for souvenirs, I struck gold! I found booklets of postcards, and although they were yellow from age, they had to suffice. Later, while Prof and the children looked at the animals in the zoo, I sat on a park bench and wrote up the cards. At a handy Post Office next door to the zoo, I mailed all of them. The card I mailed to coworkers at my office arrived three weeks after my return to Canada!

Professor Ojo took us to visit the dam that supplied water for irrigating the area. It surprised me to see herds of brown and white cows grazing in the valley close to the dam. There was scarcely any grass for them to eat. Maybe grass was there, but I didn't see it.

In the afternoon, we viewed more of the incredible mountains and boulders. The roads (or should I say tracks) through the mountains were narrow, and unkept. It seemed they were rarely used, suggesting that all this wonderful view was going to waste. No one cared a hoot about it.

We were driving slowly along the road, with visibility not more than a car length because sections had overhang from bushes, when suddenly, without an inkling, we came upon a narrow wooden bridge high above a deep ravine. We had two options; we could go forward or backward. Richard made a quick decision, and prepared to negotiate the rickety bridge. Trying not to look down, I closed my eyes and crossed myself. I'm not even Catholic! What if the wooden planks had rotted? Could the structure withstand the weight of the car with its five passengers? If our car slipped off the bridge, we would plunge several hundred feet below to our deaths. The treacherous bridge reminded me of one in an Indiana Jones movie, except it was on a smaller scale. There were no houses in the area and no signs of human life was visible. If we had any problems, it would probably be several hours before someone found us. Thoughts percolated in my head: life has been so wonderful, I've accomplished a lot, but there is so much more I want to do. Did I come all this way to Nigeria to die? Was this what this long-awaited trip was all about? Could it be that all the frustrations I'd been through to obtain a visa for Nigeria, a sign, a warning not to go? Could this be my destiny? No, no, not now, Lord! There are still so many places to visit!

Ada and Zelda exchanged nervous glances with me, and like a

sisterhood pact, we huddled in the back seat, grasping each other's hands. Richard and Prof continued their amiable chatter, and didn't seem concerned, so I held my breath and tongue, as we attempted to cross the bridge. The car moved slowly over one plank, then another and another. I waited, ears cocked to hear something snap. We swayed back and forth like a baby in a cradle as the wheels slid over the rounded logs. I listened. The car continued its bumpy climb. It felt like eternity, then nothing. Relief engulfed us when finally, we reached the other side.

We spent some time looking over more rock formations in the area. Although Jos was arid country, the area was well known for its fresh fruits and vegetables. Prof directed us to a roadside market which sold healthy looking tomatoes, onions, potatoes and even sugar cane. Joyce had apparently given Richard a list of things to buy. I watched him in action as he haggled over the price of bags of potatoes and dozens of tomatoes.

On our trip to the town no one was happier than I, for we returned via a different route. In the evening we took Prof back to his house where I reiterated my appreciation to him and his wife for their extended kindness.

When we left Jos later that day, I had great respect for Joyce's intuition. She had assessed Mabel with acute precision. I had much greater appreciation for Nigerian hospitality, a fascination for the country, and renewed appreciation for my fellow human beings.

L A G O S

*T*he idea of visiting the populous city of Lagos still tweaked my interest despite the rumours I'd heard about it. When I first arrived in Lagos, there was no opportunity to see the city. Having arrived at night, I was whisked away with Suobite by taxi to a hotel close to the airport. Early next morning I was soon whisked back to the airport where I caught a flight to Port Harcourt. Those fleeting moments weren't enough to say I had seen Lagos. I felt my trip to Nigeria wouldn't be complete without spending at least a couple of days there.

Joyce must have read my mind because one morning while having breakfast with Uche, she brought up the subject.

"Yvonne, I want to take you to Lagos for three days."

Joyce spoke quietly and slowly in her unusual accent while she sipped freshly-squeezed orange juice. "Ada has to take her SAT exams at the University of Nigeria High School in Lagos, so we can kill two birds with one stone and spend extra two days to look around and visit some friends."

"I would love that very much. It'll give me a chance to visit the KLM office to switch my flight to return home from Lagos, instead of Accra," I said.

A glob of guava jam slid off the piece of toast I was eating, and flopped onto the white tablecloth. Joyce looked at the tablecloth.

"Don't worry about it, the maid will wash it," she reassured me.

"Can't take me anywhere," I said, poking fun at myself.

Uche said, "You can go anywhere you want Yvonne, you don't have to worry about a thing, just stay away from guava jam!" We both laughed.

Joyce broke up the chatter. "Yes, we should attend to the matter regarding your ticket."

A few days earlier, Joyce and I had visited the small KLM office in Owerri to change my return flight. Their computer system was too antiquated to do anything for me. After apologizing for not being able to help, the clerk said the main office in Lagos would be able to make the change.

"I'll get to look up the Jamaican High Commissioner and my friend Carlton Sewell, the Trinidadian High Commissioner," I said. I had almost given up hope that I would see them.

"I haven't met the current Jamaican High Commissioner yet, so this will be a good opportunity to meet him. When Dudley Thompson was High Commissioner, I invited him out to visit Owerri and we had a great reception for him here," Joyce said.

"Oh, really?" This surprised me. I didn't know Joyce had time to associate with diplomats. She seemed so busy with her intellectual colleagues and the various chiefs.

"Yes, I organized the entire thing," she said.

"My wife is quite something isn't she?" Uche looked admiringly across the table at Joyce.

"Yes she is." I was impressed. "I don't know much about the new guy, but my friend, the Counsel General to Toronto gave me his name and number and suggested I call on him."

"Let's do it." Joyce sounded keen to visit the High Commissioner and that was fine with me.

She was a terrific organizer, and from comments I'd heard from her colleagues when she took me on a tour of her university, she was a wonderful Dean. In one day, she had our itinerary for Lagos organized, and one of the drivers at her disposal assigned to drive us. Joyce, Ada and I, along with the driver would make the trip the next day.

Later that evening, I was sitting on my bed reading a novel I'd found among the hundreds of books stacked into bookshelves all over the house. Joyce stuck her head through the bedroom door.

"Hi Yvonne, it's a long drive to Lagos, so please try to get a good night's rest."

"It only took forty-five minutes to fly from Lagos to Port Harcourt when I came here. How long could the drive be?" I asked with sarcasm. I was sure Joyce was exaggerating.

"About nine hours."

"Nine hours?" I repeated with disbelief.

"It's a long way from here and the roads are not the greatest," Joyce said.

I was excited to visit Lagos but that bit of information forced the wind out of my sail. I didn't want to sit for nine hours to get there, not after the previous nine hour marathon to Jos. My idea of a long drive was maximum four hours, and in a comfortable car with stereo jamming, airconditioning up high or sunroof popped wide open. I'm well endowed in the derriere area, but the buffer is definitely not designed for sitting hours on end. To make things worse, the university cars were not air conditioned or if they were, the systems were ineffective. But I had no choice, for I very much wanted to see the place I'd heard so much about.

The drive to Lagos was an endurance trip. It was a blessing that I hadn't eaten a big breakfast that morning, or I would have had difficulty retaining it within my stomach. Joyce's description that the roads were not the greatest, was an understatement. But being the optimist that I am, I hung onto the enchanting idea of a pot of gold at the end of the rainbow.

The dry season was obviously not a severe one that year, for it didn't have an adverse effect on the vegetation. The countryside was lush. Emerald wooded hills and deep grassy valleys beckoned us to go forward. Similar to Ghana, I was surprised to see many of the plants that I knew from the Caribbean. Cashew and mango trees covered in blossoms, were in abundance. There were breadfruit trees, banana trees, oil nut trees, and the indomitable palm trees. Ubiquitous cassava patches justified why fu-fu was a staple food, for it was the cassava root from which it was made. In some areas, we came upon cassava roots that were harvested, sliced into strips, and placed at the side of the road to be sun dried. Joyce explained that a kind of flour called garri was made from the dried cassava.

Adamson's bright smile came back to tantalize me, as his words echoed in my ears. "Kumasi have de best garri. Mmmm, it is de best in de world," Adamson had said as we drove passed vendors selling bags of the cream-coloured flour along the road, the day we visited Kumasi.

The trip to Lagos took us through many small towns where the local people lined the streets, selling their wares. As the Peugeot ate up the miles, we drove through several states, Anambra, Delta, Edo, Ondo, and Ogun. At Delta State we came upon a long, wide bridge. It was a bridge of stature, not quite the magnitude I expected to see in the area.

"Which river is that below?" I asked. I had crossed many rivers while touring Nigeria but they seemed like streams compared to this one.

"It's de Niger Riva," James, our driver replied.

"The mighty Niger that I read about in geography books?"

"Yes, Miss."

I was ecstatic. It was the greatest river of West Africa and the longest of the African continent. There is something euphoric about experiencing things in history and geography books. I get a rush from these experiences.

"I would love to take a picture of it."

"Don't worry, Miss," James said.

At that moment we were half way across the huge bridge. Looking through the open car windows from both left and right sides, I could see the great Niger flowing lazily below. The only clear indication of the dry season, were tiny, sedimentary islands in the river due to low water level. James pulled the car over to the left side of the road and stopped in the middle of the traffic.

"You can't do this can you, James?" I asked sheepishly.

Any moment I expected policemen to appear, ready to charge us with an offence. Joyce and Ada sat calmly in the car, unperturbed, admiring the view.

"Don't worry about me, just take yuh picture," James replied.

He got out of the car and put the hood up. I laughed and winked at him as I realized the ploy. I took photographs leisurely from both sides of the bridge. As far as my eyes could focus, the Niger looked gray and mysterious. It was a view worth capturing on camera. After I took several pictures, James put the hood down and we continued our journey.

The road to Lagos was dotted with military blockades as were all the roads that I travelled in Nigeria. Seeing the soldiers jarred my memory and brought back my first encounter with the soldier on the road to Owerri. Thank goodness, this time I was with Joyce, I felt safe.

I watched as groups of soldiers with their weapons drawn, randomly pull over vehicles, anticipating our turn any moment. That moment never came, and after we'd pass several checkpoints without being stopped, I tapped Joyce on her shoulder as she sat in the front of the car.

"Aren't we lucky? They haven't pulled us over once."

"It's not really luck," Joyce said.

"Oh really? Why do you say that?"

"We're driving in a Federal University car, with the name printed on the side."

"So? What does that have to do with anything?" It seemed Joyce knew something I didn't.

"It's an unwritten rule that the soldiers do not interfere with Federal vehicles," Joyce explained.

"Well, isn't that too bad! If I had that privilege the afternoon when I travelled from Port Harcourt to Owerri, I would've avoided the encounter with the gold-tooth soldier, especially since I'd just arrived in the country."

"I know," Joyce empathized. "I'm sorry about your ordeal. Chalk it up to one of life's experiences." She turned to look at me.

I looked at the soldiers. They were strong, strapping men.

"What a waste of manpower to have all these able-bodied men hanging around on the streets. The government should utilize them to do something constructive like repairing the roads."

"I hardly think that will happen," Joyce said.

I imagined our journey would have lasted an additional two or three hours if we had been pulled over at each blockade. Nine hours later, we continued to zigzag across the country as James negotiated huge pot holes along the way. The roads could be aptly described as an obstacle course. The difference being, we were not playing a game.

It was early evening when I began to sense that the quiet country roads were no longer quiet. Miles and miles of uniformed greenery were now interspersed more frequently with houses and office buildings. Then I heard it: a hum, kind of like a mummer, a distant sound. I listened intently as we got closer and closer. The sound became louder and louder. I felt it in the air, a feeling of vibrancy, of activity, of movement.

We had reached the city of Lagos, a sprawling mass of urbanism lay before us. Similar to New York, the city is built on islands. I could see snippets of ocean in between the buildings and bridges. Located at the southwestern tip of Nigeria, Lagos borders on the Atlantic ocean. Multi-lane highways crisscrossed each other over concrete bridges giving the city a New York atmosphere, yet looking nothing like New

York. The spectacular National Theatre building gleamed in the distance, a noticeable piece of architecture. A mixture of high-rise and low-rise buildings, many needing a paint job, came into view.

Finally, we were in the heart of Lagos. It didn't take long to understand why it is one of Africa's most populous cities. Thousands of people were moving about everywhere. Traffic moved like turtles on the sea shore. A mob of panhandlers descended upon our car and all others in the queue like a flock of vultures attacking a dead carcass. Scared to death, I clutched my purse, wondering if I should try to hide it under the seat, but the look of confidence on Joyce and Ada's face helped to calm my nerves. Young children competed ferociously with adults as they rushed against cars, trying to sell their wares, from board games to plastic bags of water. While some looked healthy, others looked starved and undernourished. I was astonished at the number of young children involved in panhandling activity, especially since it was a Friday, and a school day. Slowly, carefully, James managed to drive through the seemingly crazy mass of people and entered a more sedate part of town.

— ◇ —

Before long we arrived at the gates of the University of Nigeria. Joyce showed the guards her business card. They looked us over, then allowed our car to enter the gates. It was a large campus with several faculty buildings. The senate building, an imposing structure, stood several stories high in the centre of the complex. One of the guards directed our driver to park close to the main university building. Joyce led the way to the university hotel which was housed in one wing of the campus.

When Joyce inquired about accommodation for three, (the drivers always slept in the car) the receptionist promptly told her there were no rooms available, the hotel was fully booked. But Joyce was no push over, and demanded to see the hotel manager. The receptionist quickly disappeared to a back room. A few minutes later, she returned with a middle age sturdily-built woman who looked like a drill sergeant. She marched over to Joyce with a quizzical look on her face. Before Joyce opened her mouth, she spoke.

"We have no vacant rooms for this weekend Madame."

"Mrs? ... I didn't get your name," Joyce said as she rummaged through her purse.

"Mrs. Olo," the manager replied, her voice oozing with self-confidence.

Joyce retrieved one of her business cards from the purse and handed it to Mrs. Olo.

"I'm Joyce Ombede, wife of Vice Chancellor Uche Ombede at Owerri University. I hope you can help us?" Mrs Olo looked at the business card, at Joyce, then at the rest of us standing at the counter, and her expression softened.

"Come with me," she said. She collected a set of keys from among several hanging on the wall behind the counter, and personally escorted us across a long walkway to a second floor, to suite 2B. She opened the door to the suite, ushered us in, then explained how everything worked. "This is the best accommodation I can find for you at such short notice Dr. Ombede. I hope you and your party will be comfortable." She sounded apologetic. Joyce looked around the small compact suite. It was clean with two double beds, a dresser, table and small refrigerator.

"This will do just fine for overnight. Thank you, Mrs. Olo."

Taking her hand, Joyce shook it. Mrs. Olo left the room quietly, and Ada and I jumped on one of the beds and burst out laughing.

"Say Joyce, nothing like pulling rank eh?" I asked playfully. But Joyce was very serious and shrugged it off.

"They always have room for special people if you deal with the manager."

Who would know that more than I do? As a bank manager, I've on many occasions satisfied my client's wishes after a junior staff had insisted certain things couldn't be done. It is always a matter of weighing the pros and the cons and making a judgement call. It's a common belief that junior staff members are not paid enough to think. Maybe they're right.

We spent a restful Friday night at the University of Nigeria Hotel, so that Ada wouldn't be tired or late for her SAT examinations the next day.

After a leisurely breakfast in the hotel's restaurant Saturday morning, I sat on a chair under a covered walkway observing the students as they moved about. The campus grounds seemed conducive to studying with grassy stretches and in-ground park benches. A canal ran behind the property and beyond it was a great view of the city. Slender palm trees swayed in the wind that blew off the Atlantic.

Suddenly, I saw movement in the square concrete garden a few feet in front of me. Most of the flowers that were planted in it had dried up and the few remaining ones were unkept, but there was some other life-form in the garden. A large lizard was crawling along one side of the wall, trying to get out. It had an orange coloured head and tail with a dark coloured body. I fished the camera from my handbag and quickly took a picture of it. It was the same specie as the one I'd seen in Joyce's yard. I thought it would be good evidence for mother-in-law to backup her concern and confirm to her that "lizards are down there" just as she had feared.

— ✧ —

As soon as Ada completed her SAT examinations, we cleared out of the university hotel. Joyce directed James and soon we were driving through a quiet part of town. The streets were orderly with charming houses painted in pastel shades. Uniformed hedges of variegated croton of yellow, green and red, enveloped the houses and bougainvillaeas sprouted throughout the gardens. It could have been a middle-class area in any of the Caribbean Islands.

After winding through the residential area, we drove through a commercial part of town where dignified architecture graced the skyline and charming storefronts invited us in, displaying designer goods like Gucci and Calvin Klein.

Soon we were climbing a small mound to a palatial building several stories high. James stopped in front of the building and two uniformed bellboys sprang forward to open the doors for us.

Joyce booked us into the Federal Palace Hotel. Now this was more my speed. Large, modern, upscale, it had all the pomp and pageantry of a five star hotel. Once we completed our registration, a bellboy escorted us to the elevator and ushered us along a wide corridor covered with plush, green carpet to our suite on the eighth floor. It was spacious with high ceilings, brocaded drapes and elegant mahogany furniture. I noticed the sliding doors at once, threw them open, and stepped onto the wide balcony. The salty Atlantic air tickled my nose as I took in the fabulous view. I stared across the ocean inlet to parts of Lagos on another island. The ocean looked inviting, a shimmering kaleidoscope of varying shades of blue. Several luxury boats cruised by, their passengers gayly absorbing the hot African sunlight.

Later that day, Joyce and I visited the KLM office to exchange my return ticket so that I could depart from Lagos instead of Accra. When the KLM personnel informed me emphatically, that this could not be done, I knew I should have strangled Mohammed, my travel agent. If I hadn't before, I was now convinced that he was born and kept alive, just to cause me grief. Did that young man have the right information on anything? So far, everything he'd told me was incorrect. The news was upsetting. Since I couldn't do anything to Mohammed at that moment, and believe me, I thought of a few things, I accepted Joyce's help and counsel. I regained my composure and conceded that I would have to fly back to Accra in order to return home to Canada. When I thought about it afterwards, it dawned on me that it wasn't such a bad idea, maybe, just maybe, I would get to see Adamson once more.

Our next mission was to visit the Jamaican High Commissioner to Lagos. I gave Joyce the address and she directed our driver on how to get there. At the High Commissioner's office, a gateman took our cards and asked us to wait while he disappeared behind a high metal fence. After a few minutes he reappeared smiling and invited us in. An aide ushered us into a spacious sitting room advising us that the High Commissioner would see us soon. In a short while the High Commissioner came forward to greet us.

We had a pleasant visit with him and when he asked us to return that night to a previously planned private dinner party, we accepted his invitation eagerly.

That evening, Joyce and I had leisurely baths as we luxuriated in perfumed bubbles. We polished our nails, then got all dolled up. It was my first opportunity to dress semi-formally since arriving in Africa as all my outings had been casual so far.

We had invited Ada along but she wasn't interested. Joyce rented videos from the hotel's store, and ordered room service to be sent to her. Ada was in her element. Being alone to watch videos and eat good food in a fancy hotel, was just what the doctor ordered. No doubt, it was more exciting than listening to the constant banter between her mother and me.

The dinner party was a pleasurable evening with interesting guests. The meal was scrumptious, undoubtedly influenced by the French cuisine of the High Commissioner's Haitian wife.

She murdered the English language when communicating with us. All the guests smiled sympathetically when she tried to explain something in English.

"My English not so good, ya?" she asked, looking around the table with large imploring brown eyes.

"You're doing just fine," Joyce replied quickly hoping to put her at ease.

"The shrimp casserole is lovely. Did you make it yourself?" I asked. I hadn't seen evidence of a housekeeper since we arrived.

"Yes, I cook it. I cook everything. 'Ow you say it? the 'ousekeeper off today."

"You must have spent all day preparing this," another guest said.

By this time, all eyes were focused on the High Commissioner's wife for she had put on quite a spread, rice and peas, shrimp salad, shrimp casserole, steamed fish, spicy chicken in a cream sauce, tossed salad, candid yams and more. Exquisite china and crystal graced the large dining table, accentuated by delicate linen serviettes.

"Oh, Robert 'elped me." She beamed and looked lovingly at her husband.

"My wife is too modest; she really did all the work. I only helped to cut up the vegetables."

Later, we adjourned to the spacious living room where we sipped liqueurs from delicate Waterford crystal. Several conversations ensued between small groups. Two guests were pilots who flew domestic flights across Nigeria and they shared some of their experiences with us. We burst out laughing when John, a handsome thirty-year-old pilot, stated that he was afraid of heights.

"Come on John, you must be joking. How can a pilot, flying aeroplanes thousands of feet up in the sky be afraid of heights?" Tom, a gynaecologist, asked with sarcasm.

"Don't ask me how it works. I don't know. All I know is, once I'm in that cockpit, and there is something over my head, the fear disappears." John gave his answer so honestly that the group accepted it. Still, I thought it incredible and hoped I never had to fly with him.

Madge, a Jamaican native and a dentist, who was married to Tom, the Nigerian gynaecologist, struck up a conversation with me. She had lived in Nigeria for twenty-seven years.

"I'm really happy to see how your sister is wearing the African clothes; she must have adjusted to the African way of life," Madge said as she glanced at Joyce.

While everyone at the dinner party wore western style clothing, including the Nigerians, Joyce wore an African outfit. Most of the time while I was in Nigeria, Joyce wore African clothing. Tonight, she wore an angle length dress in beige, red and green diagonal stripes. The bodice was low cut and trimmed with stripes of the same colours as were the large puff sleeves. Two layers of frills hugged her hips and a matching small headpiece framed her head. She accentuated the dress with a pair of red shoes. The outfit was quite becoming. I looked at Joyce in the far corner of the room and smiled. The clothing enhanced her tall, slim figure and with her long aristocratic neck, she looked very graceful.

"What about you? You have not adjusted?" I asked, surprised at Madge's comments.

"My dear, I don't think I'll ever adjust fully to this place. My mother-in-law and my husband's family used to interfere a lot in my life, but I don't get involved with them anymore. I just want to be left alone to enjoy my family and life."

I smiled as she reminded me of Greta Garbo's famous words in *Grand Hotel*, "I vant to be alone." Madge looked just as wistful as Garbo. I could tell from her comments and the tone of her voice, Madge wasn't happy. I thought twenty-seven years was a long time to be in a relationship. Whatever her predicament, I supposed she decided to stick it out. The chatter created from new friendships brought laughter that continued far into the early hours of the next morning. Finally, the guests began to disperse. Joyce and I thanked the High Commissioner and his wife for a delightful dinner and a pleasant evening. They called a cab and we returned to our hotel just before the cocks began to crow.

The next day I was in for a surprise. When I arrived at Carlton Sewell's office, the High Commissioner for Trinidad to Lagos, I learned that he was no longer in Lagos. He'd been reassigned to Brussels. Well, isn't that something? I thought. It was good that my original plan to spend a week in Lagos had changed, for I'd planned to spend some of my time with Carlton and his family. With one less person to visit, I spent the rest of Sunday socializing with Joyce's friends. We visited several West Indians. They all lived monogamously in big houses and seemed to be doing well.

I found one person particularly interesting. Mr. Ekwue was a banker like myself, but that was as far as the similarities went. It was obvious from the large sprawling house and the four foreign cars, including a late model Mercedes Benz parked in the driveway, he was wealthy. I thought my cosy three bedroom house in Toronto's suburbs was about average size, but Mr. Ekwue's living room was the size of my entire first floor! The furniture and rugs were exquisite. Yes, thought I, my African brothers and sisters live well when they live well. He was by no means a snob. He was a humble, soft spoken man. His wife Mary, was a pleasant attractive woman. She quickly brought us refreshments. Before long, she was engrossed in a conversation with Joyce. I struck up a conversation with Mr. Ekwue about banking in Nigeria and soon we were comparing the banking systems of both our countries. Despite my pledge to avoid work-related discussions, this was too irresistible to pass up. The banking industry in Nigeria was experiencing major problems at the time, and several large banks had failed, with widespread corruption cited as the main cause.

A photograph of Mr. and Mrs Ekwue and their two daughters, which hung from the living room wall, caught my attention. They were all dressed in black and white striped costumes. Later, as I leafed through photo albums, while he narrated the events in the pictures, I again saw pictures of him and his family dressed in the same costumes. Mr Ekwue stated that he was from the Tiv tribe, and that I'd seen their traditional Tiv costume. I remembered professor Ojo and the day we visited the gift shop in Jos when he had us both dressed in Tiv costumes. I recognized the material in the photographs as similar.

"Where are your daughters now?" I asked.

"They are away in England, studying."

This did not surprise me, for by now, I'd observed that all the well-to-do Nigerians I'd met, sent their children to study either in England or the United States. Joyce had done the same with her first son.

"I want you to stop at my house for refreshments on the day when you're leaving Nigeria," Mr. Ekwue offered. "I will personally take you to the airport that day."

"Thank you so much for offering. I look forward to seeing you again." I felt genuine warmth flowing from him.

I couldn't fathom the kindness of so many of the African brothers I'd met in Ghana and Nigeria. Everyone wanted to help me and with no strings attached! Did this have anything to do with me personally? Could this be the answer to the question I've asked myself many times? "What was it about the African people that allowed them to be forced into slavery?" Was it their easy trust and unconditional kindness? No, this is too simple, it can't be the answer. I'll have to explore it deeper.

I left Mr. Ekwue's home anticipating seeing him and his wife again, but the second visit to his home did not occur.

After Joyce, Ada and I had explored Lagos and visited all of Joyce's West Indian friends in the city, we returned to Owerri. Somehow the return trip was not as arduous as the trip to Lagos. Maybe because the anxiety to reach our destination had been appeased, or maybe I had overcome the deep fear based on my perception of a terrible place, because the journey was still nine hours.

— ◇ —

Back in Owerri, while looking over my travel documents, the realization dawned on me that I had two days less than originally planned, because I had to return via Accra to get home. Joyce had planned trips for me to visit Abuja, Nigeria's new Federal capital, the Game Reserve and Uche's village. The trip to the Game Reserve would have compensated admirably for a safari, but this was not to be. Regrettably, we had to cancel these trips. Again I could have strangled Mohammed. Not being able to visit these places because of time constraint was disappointing, but I was later soothed by the wise words of my loving grandmother Eliza, "Every disappointment is for a good."

Those words didn't make sense to me as a child, but they make a lot of sense to me now.

What good could come from all this? They were major landmarks to visit and stand in the spiritual environment of history. They were a part of Nigeria's culture. I concluded, it could be something to look forward to and good reason to visit the country another time. Forget that I told the gold-tooth soldier that I would never return to his country.

*M*y last few hours in Owerri came all too soon. The days had appeared and disappeared like the scenery through the window of a moving train. Sometimes it seemed as if I were watching a movie, it appeared so unreal. I'd become accustomed to the rhythm of Joyce and Uche's routine and looked forward to our suppertime tete-a-tete. The household helpers had tripped over themselves to take care of all my needs, always service with big bright smiles.

The children loved to spend time with me in the back living room where we shared stories. Ada's stories were always revealing. On one occasion, we talked about religion.

"I see a lot of banners all over the towns advertising different Christian churches. I didn't know Nigerians were so religious," I said, trying to get a better understanding of this aspect of life.

"About 49 percent of the population are Christians and 41 percent are Muslims, but the rest are what we call African God Worshippers" Ada said.

"Really? I had no idea the Muslim religion was so widespread here, but tell me a little about the African God Worshippers." I was surprised and fascinated with the information. Growing up in the Caribbean, Christianity was all I knew.

"Basically, before Arabs brought the Muslim religion here and Europeans brought Christianity, Nigerians worshipped their own gods. They had gods for many things. That tradition is still practised today."

Certain cultural things began to make sense. "So having more than one wife would be acceptable in the Muslim culture then?" I was thinking about the discussions my friends and I used to have about this topic.

"Yes, they can have up to four wives and the African God Worshippers can have as many as they can afford, but Christians are monogamous."

"How does Christianity affect the local culture?" I was truly fascinated.

"Many of them are religious all right, but when push comes to shove, religion goes out the door and culture reigns," Ada said.

She always seemed more mature than her eighteen years. I could always rely on her for candid answers to my questions

Zelda loved to rest her head on my lap while I told them about Canada. I also told them stories about Jamaica, the country of their mother's and maternal grandmother's birth, the country they had never been. From what I gathered, the children were totally submerged in the African culture, and there were no plans for them to visit Jamaica now or in the near future. I thought it rather ironic that I, who was born and raised in Jamaica, had been so determined to visit the land of my ancestors, several generations and centuries removed. On the other hand, Joyce's children, who were born in Africa and were one generation removed, seemed to have no knowledge of or interest in the land of their mother's birth. Perhaps the desire to explore the other side of their heritage would develop later.

Before setting out for Port Harcourt airport to catch a flight to Lagos, I re-wrapped the mother-and-child carving that I had bought in Ghana, in thick brown paper. It would be carried in my arms as I'd done twice before.

In preparation for my departure, I looked around the Ombedes' house for the last time. It had been a marvellous visit. It was the place where I'd experienced much peace and tranquillity, the place where I'd learned so much about Nigerian culture.

I said a sad goodbye to all the household helpers with handshakes seasoned with a few nairas and heard their once cheerful greeting, "You're welcome," for the last time. Today, however, there was nothing cheerful about those words. The children hugged and kissed me. Zelda clung to me with tears in her eyes, and asked if I would return. I assured her I would, but not immediately. James shook my hand and said he'd see me in America. My feminine intuition told me to take that comment seriously. During my stay in his home, I'd observed that he was more American than the Yankees. He was the modern day Don Quixote, living in a fantasy land of America. He even tried to speak like an American! His dream, his obsession, was to join his older brother in America, to study. I turned over in my mind the words I would say to my mother-in-law. For her, I had a positive report about Owerri. It would fulfill the promise I'd made to myself. I would assure her that her daughter and grandchildren were indeed okay. No starvation or lack of necessities here, and Joyce had no concerns about lizards.

Joyce and I travelled in one car while Uche and Chinedu, his personal assistant, followed behind in another. Both cars were driven by chauffeurs. Joyce instructed the driver to divert from the airport road, to allow us to collect two Nigerian outfits that were being custom made for me.

My thoughts took me back to shopping with Joyce when I'd bought two pieces of dress materials. She'd taken me to two of her dressmakers the same day, and had assured me the outfits would be ready before I left the country. One dressmaker was a woman with a small shop on the second floor of a building which housed stores and offices in downtown Owerri. Lucy, was a pretty, stylish Nigerian woman with large breasts and a behind you could sit on and not fall off. Hands with crimson-red painted fingernails thrust a magazine containing dozens of Nigerian fashions at me. Lucy told me to select one. I soon found a style I liked, and showed it to her. She warned me that that particular style would emphasize my derriere. Knowing that I had more than enough there (but not as much as Lucy), I certainly didn't want to highlight it. I quickly chose another style. Lucy approved, and asked me for a deposit which I promptly paid. I was impressed with her professionalism and felt confident everything would be okay.

Before we left the shop, I heard Joyce warning Lucy to have the dress ready on time for pick up before I left the country. When we returned to our car, I looked at Joyce inquiringly.

"Joyce, you sounded as if you were threatening poor Lucy."

"You don't understand these people, Yvonne. When you tell them one week, you are lucky if they get the job done in one month. It's okay if you live here and have time, but I realize it is important for you to have the dress on time. That is why I'm not asking her to make both dresses."

We left Lucy's shop and Joyce directed our driver to another dressmaking establishment about three miles away. This time the dressmaker was a man. Joyce introduced me to Charles, a young man, about twenty-five years old, and a native Ghanaian.

"Hello Charles, nice to meet you," I said, as I shook his hand. "I was in your country a week ago. It is lovely."

"You were in Ghana?" he asked, surprised. He had a pronounced Ghanaian accent. By now I found it easier to differentiate between the Ghanaian and Nigerian accents.

"Yes, I had a great time there. Your people are so friendly, I felt at home."

Adamson's smiling face danced in front of me. I could almost reach out and touch him, he seemed so real. I tried to focus on Charles as he beamed proudly at me.

"Yes, we're good people," Charles said.

"How on earth did you end up being a dressmaker in Nigeria?" I asked, remembering Pearl, the young dressmaker who'd made me a lovely outfit in Ghana.

"It's a long story, but a lot of people migrate from Ghana to Nigeria to find work. Bigger country you know."

Charles took my measurements, touching me ever so delicately. I wondered if somehow, without my knowledge, a sign was etched on my forehead which said, "fragile, handle with care." After he finished measuring, we discussed the style I wanted. It was similar to one of Joyce's dresses that I'd fallen in love with. Joyce had brought the dress along.

"How would you like the headpiece?" Charles asked.

"Oh, I don't know. You chose something for me, but something that I can tie myself without much trouble."

Having seen many elaborate headpieces worn by Nigerian women, I knew there was an art in tying them properly. Since I wasn't versed in the art and I knew no one in Toronto to help me with it, I opted for simple.

"All right, I may have to give it out, but I'll get them to make something nice for you."

Joyce stressed the importance of having the outfit made and ready for pickup in a week's time, and Charles promised it would be ready—on time.

— ✧ —

We arrived first at Lucy's shop. She was still working on the dress! The sleeves were not yet sewn in, the hem of the skirt remained to be done and the general trimming of the garment was still unfinished.

Joyce was angry. To save some time, I suggested we visit Charles to collect the other outfit, then return to Lucy's shop. Hopefully on our return, Lucy would have the garment ready. We sped to Charles's shop, leaving Uche and his driver to wait at the side of the road. You guessed it. Charles hadn't completed the dress. He told us he still had to collect the headpiece. Seeing the distressed look on my face, he asked his assistant to go down the street to collect the headpiece immediately. Charles worked diligently at putting the finishing touches on the dress. Within half an hour, he had stitched, trimmed, ironed and folded the dress, then placed it in a plastic bag. The assistant returned during that time with the headpiece and Charles placed it also in the plastic bag. I thanked him, paid the balance owing, and Joyce and I dashed back to our car.

The driver was fast asleep at the wheel while the car idled in front of Charles's shop. Joyce shook him by the shoulder. He opened bloodshot eyes, and stared at us as if he'd seen a ghost.

"Wake up, man; you have a job to do," Joyce snapped.

"Sorry Miss Ombede, I'm a little tired today," the driver said.

"Let's go, man; we have to get back to Lucy's shop and we're running out of time."

Although usually soft spoken, Joyce could be very authoritarian at times. I've seen the helpers scatter when she appears at certain times.

Luckily, Lucy's shop was a short distance away. When we returned the outfit was still not ready. We waited impatiently until Lucy completed the job. It was a close call. There wasn't time to try on any of the outfits or to pack them neatly. I stuffed the dresses hurriedly, like packing groceries in a shopping bag, into my suitcase from the trunk of the car. I kissed Joyce and Uche goodbye from the side of the road at 10:00 a.m. and headed for Port Harcourt airport.

The plan was to fly domestic from Port Harcourt to Logos, then catch another flight from Lagos to Accra. Uche had arranged to have his driver chauffeur me to Port Harcourt Airport while he returned home with Joyce. He'd also assigned Chinedu to accompany me. Chinedu was a brilliant, twenty-five year old man who spoke excellent English. He was dressed in a navy blue suit and a white shirt. I thought he was overdressed for the occasion but I made no comments.

Upon our arrival we were told there were no flights to Lagos that afternoon. The sky had become very hazy because of the Harmattan, and no flights were permitted to take off. I was suddenly in a quandary. I had to get to Accra to catch my flight to Amsterdam by 1:00 p.m. the next day. If I missed it, I would have to pay a full fare to get home to Toronto. Chinedu must have seen the panic on my face because he took me aside.

"Miss Blackwood, I don't want you to worry." He spoke with a calm, reassuring tone. "The V. C. thought of this possibility and told me we should drive you to Lagos, if there are no flights."

"Oh thank you, Chinedu. You are all wonderful. I don't know what I would do if I couldn't get to Lagos." I knew God was still on my side; I felt it in my soul that things would work out.

This time the thought of a nine-hour drive was of no concern. My preoccupation was to get to Lagos. The journey would be eleven hours instead of nine because we'd travelled south to Port Harcourt and must now go north, then west to Lagos.

Although we stopped only once to change a flat tire, put gas in the car, and purchase something to drink, the trip seemed like forever. From the back seat of the car, I watched the light from the blazing sun lazily disappear. Darkness closed its huge gloved hand over our path as figures dissolved into the shadows. Pitch darkness covered the land. So black was the night, Vampire bats would require bifocals to see! Visibility was no more than an arm's length, and only by looking directly into the path created by the headlights. Peripheral vision was zilch. Fear gripped me and kept me harnessed the rest of the journey, fear that any moment, the driver would hit an object in the road before he could see it, fear that we could be easily ambushed by thieves in the night. Silently, I prayed many short, spasmodic prayers, having perfected the art since my arrival in Nigeria. Remembering my chance meeting with Reverend Suobite, I wondered if he had anything to do with it.

I was surprised to see that police checkpoints continued to operate in the darkness. Each post was lit by kerosene lanterns and torches as the soldiers pulled over cars and trucks late into the night.

After much anxiety and prayers, we arrived in Lagos without mishap. It was almost midnight. We were tired, hungry, and dirty. My plan to visit the kindhearted banker, Mr. Ekwue, dissipated for it was too late to barge in on him.

With little choice, we checked into Ikeja Palace Hotel. It was definitely not a palace. A mediocre hotel, it had one thing in its favour; it was near the airport. I offered to pay for Chinedu and the driver's rooms, a small compensation for dragging them all the way to Lagos. Anxious to put some nutrition in our bodies, we asked the receptionist for direction to the hotel's restaurant. She looked at us as if we each had two heads, then informed us that the hotel's kitchen was closed for the night. With heavy hearts, we went to our beds—hungry.

That night, sleep eluded me. My stomach gurgled and growled so loudly, I was convinced the guests next door could hear it. I tried to suppress the noise by lying on one of the fluffy foam pillows! Eventually, sleep came calling. With the pillow firmly wedged between my stomach and the mattress, the call was answered.

I awoke early next morning and after washing, I dressed and went to bang on Chinedu's door. He opened the door with sleep-filled eyes. I asked him to wake up the driver.

Anticipating a big, healthy breakfast before going to the airport, the three of us hurried to the hotel's restaurant. We waited almost an hour for the kitchen staff to arrive, but they did not show up. Time was limited and not knowing what the flight schedules to Accra were, we couldn't wait around any longer. We set out for the airport without food; we were famished. I thought of the Federal Palace Hotel where Joyce, Ada and I had stayed. Management would never have allowed something like this to happen there. If the regular staff didn't show up on time, there would have been a backup plan to facilitate the guests. Oh well, you get what you pay for, I always say. If Ikeja Palace had any stars behind its name, they should be erased, in my opinion.

When we arrived at the airport, I dashed to the check-in counter, with the driver and Chinedu at my heels, to ask about flights to Accra. I learned that a 9:00 a.m. flight was scheduled. Oh thank you Jesus; everything is going to be just fine. Noting the long queue already formed, I could tell it would be a full flight. I joined it quickly for I had no intentions of missing that flight. Timing would be perfect. I would arrive in Accra by 10:00 a.m., three hours before the departure of my KLM flight to Amsterdam.

While standing in the queue, waiting for my turn to purchase a ticket, I began to feel hot and uncomfortable. Beads of perspiration broke out on my forehead. I pulled a handkerchief from by purse and mopped my face. Suddenly, it became unbearably hot. The ceiling fans revolved slowly overhead, but they didn't seem to help. A black shadow began to creep in on me from the sides. The light, oh God, the light, it was being eaten up by the shadow. The airport began to look smaller and smaller. The people in the queues around me shrank into midgets, and instead of talking, they whispered. What's happening to me, I'm shrinking! I tried to wave my hands frantically, but they felt like lead. In slow motion I saw Chinedu moving toward me. Before I could speak, he was just in time to catch me as total darkness engulfed me.

In the world of darkness, time stands still. Nothing moves, neither forward nor backward. You are suspended, lurking in another place. I couldn't say for how long I was out, but I was revived with a splash of cold water. Chinedu led me away to find food, while my driver held my spot in the queue. I realized then, that I hadn't contracted any strange disease! I simply hadn't eaten in twenty-three hours.

We found a small snack counter in the airport and bought sandwiches and tea. Sitting at the counter with my feet dangling from a high stool, I wolfed down the food. I felt the wonderful nourishment, anything would have been wonderful, move slowly down to my empty dehydrated stomach. The growling and gurgling I'd suffered through the night before, began a repeat performance. Before long, my strength returned, and I felt alive again. Chinedu ate slowly like a gentleman. When I almost toppled off the high stool, in my haste to return to the ticket counter, he promptly shoved the rest of the sandwich in his mouth and gulped down half a cup of tea. We returned to the queue and relieved the driver of his post giving him an opportunity to also eat.

My turn came to be processed and I moved up to the counter. I handed the clerk my passport and asked for a ticket to Accra. She told me the price and I handed her some visa traveller's cheques after signing them. She looked at me as if I was a crazy woman, then informed me that she couldn't take travellers' cheques for payment. I had several thousand Nairas in my purse, so I offered those.

"I can't take local currency from you because you are travelling on a Canadian passport," the clerk said.

"What do you mean? I am here in your country, and this is your currency and you won't take it?"

What was that thing I'd learned in college about money and banking? Yes, yes, legal tender. What about legal tender, I thought. She probably never heard the terminology, so I won't confuse her.

"No, you have to pay by American dollars," she said firmly.

"Look, the traveller's cheques are in American dollars, and they are accepted all over the world. Why can't you take them?"

Travelling in Africa had taught me some interesting things; one, that travellers' cheques may be safe in terms of theft, they had saved my hide when the soldier on the road to Owerri searched my bags, but they are a pain in the butt to exchange, and when you find someone who will take them, they take a percentage for service charge. In Ghana, sometimes it was as much as five percent.

"Sorry I can't take them. Please stand aside Miss, you're holding up the line," the clerk said with a note of dismissal.

I was desperate now. I wasn't going to allow a clerk to dismiss me. This was one time I wouldn't play the role of a quiet ordinary tourist. I saw images of myself running after the aeroplane as it sped down the runway, only to take off leaving me standing, gazing into the sky. Then came the realization that I was stuck in the dreaded city of Lagos with no one to help me and with little money since I'd spent most of what I had, except the nairas. No, I have to get on this flight come hell or high water.

"Please, get your boss and let's see what can be done. I have to get on this flight," I said with a note of authority. I stood adamantly in my spot at the counter.

I felt like I was fighting for my life. Why does something like this have to happen to me now? Have I not had enough complications with this trip already? Can I not leave in peace without incident?

"Okay, but my boss is not here now," the clerk said. When I gave her the look of terror, she added, "I'll get him on the cellular phone."

She made the call while I stood aside. Chinedu and the driver, who were standing in the background, dashed over to find out what was going on. They had become very protective of me. I suspected Chinedu didn't want to have to report anything bad to his boss, the Vice Chancellor. He wanted to prove that he'd carried out his assignment well. I told them about the problem. I waited twenty minutes and the clerk did not get back to me. In the meantime, the line had dwindled to a few. Chinedu suggested that I speak to the clerk again.

"Miss, the flight must be almost full now and you haven't told me what is happening. Can you call your boss again?"

She called him again, and this time, I demanded to speak to him

on the cellular phone. I explained the situation to him and he agreed
to accept the traveller's cheques. If anxiety was a recipe for losing
weight, I had found the magic formula, for I was sure I'd lost twenty
pounds in less than two hours.

Later, when I said goodbye to Chinedu and the driver I tipped
them excessively from the extra nairas which was of no use to me
anymore. I hoped it compensated them for all the aggravation I'd put
them through. They even managed to smile when I waved goodbye
from the departure gate.

Just before noon, I touched the soil of Ghana once more, and my
thoughts were filled to overflowing with Adamson. I'd thought about
him many times during my stay in Nigeria, but had fought the idea of
phoning or writing him. I'd asked myself this question. "Why disturb
Adamson and get his hope up when you know there isn't much you can
do for him?" I'd answered the question myself, and based on the
answer had resisted the temptation. But something was playing with
my emotions. Fate had led me back to his country with a couple of
hours to spare. As it turned out, I had three hours, because the flight
to Amsterdam was delayed by another two hours. Should I call him?
Should we meet? Should I leave him alone? I'd formulated a partial
answer to these questions while waiting in the immigration queue.

I walked up to the immigration officer at the counter and handed
him my passport. He looked at me, flipped through the passport, then
he looked at me again. Actually, he stared at me.

The officer said, "Just a minute, Miss."

He left his post, taking my passport with him, and went to speak
with another officer at the far end of the room. They spoke for a short
while, then both came over to me. The second officer asked me to
follow him behind the counter. I obeyed. He ushered me into a small
windowless room and told me to have a seat. He closed the door then
picked up my passport from the desk where he'd thrown it.

"What is this all about?" I asked the immigration officer. I felt as
if I'd committed a terrible crime but didn't know what it was.

"You came into Ghana with no reentry visa. How did you get in?"
the officer asked in a stern voice.

This was such a shock to me the blood supply to my brain stopped
instantly because I felt my head become light. I was floating. A chill ran

through my body from the top of my head to the sole of my feet. The stuffy room with no ventilation, felt like a prison. Oh God, I prayed, don't let me faint again. Twice in one day can't be good for the soul! Slowly, I took a couple deep breaths, allowing the oxygen to filter to my brain cells, then choosing my words carefully, I answered the officer.

"I have to depart to Amsterdam from Ghana in order to get home to Toronto. See, here is my plane ticket." I pulled out my ticket to show him the evidence. "Let me explain ... "

After I explained the situation about the visa to Nigeria and my having to return to Ghana in order to get home, he accepted the story.

"You can't leave the airport though. I will have someone escort you with your luggage to pay departure tax, then take you to the waiting lounge."

He let me go and I breathed a sigh of relief. Another immigration personnel escorted me to pay the tax and then to the lounge. While I sat on the comfortable airport couch, I decided ... enough already, I'll leave Adamson alone.

As we travelled along the snow-covered highway, it was 6:00 p.m. on a cold February evening, but in my mind it was 11:00 p.m. It would take me a few days to readjust to the time difference. I made small talk with Martin, a friend who'd picked me up at the Toronto International Airport. I asked about the weather, politics, developments in the Afro-Canadian community and the economy. Martin readily brought me up-to-date on all topics.

"Yvonne, you certainly chose the right time to go on vacation. The week you left was the coldest Canada ever experienced in about fifty years!"

"Well, I am glad I did something right. Can you imagine that hours ago I was in temperatures of over 90 degrees?"

While we travelled along the highway, Martin kept glancing at me at intervals. I wondered why, but said nothing.

Finally, he spoke, "You know, Yvonne, something is very odd about you."

"What is it? Why do you say that?" I asked, concerned about his remark.

"You look like you're not all here. Did you leave your spirit in Africa?" he asked.

For the first time since I'd known Martin, I really looked at him. He was more perceptive than I gave him credit for. At that moment, I had a strong desire to commune with my grandmother, Eliza, to thank her for shaping me into the woman I had become. Tears welled up in my eyes.

"I don't know what it is, but you're right. I feel like I left a part of me there," I replied.

If only you knew about the fabulous adventure I've lived the past weeks ... if only you knew. Eight years ago, when I'd plucked up every ounce of courage possible and taken my son on Space Mountain, the ultimate roller coaster ride at Disney World, I'd thought that the thrill could never ever be repeated or surpassed, that never again would I experience such exhilaration, such awe—I thought wrong ... if only you knew Martin.

The car turned onto my street and I craned my neck to see my house. Despite Martin's description of the recent cold weather, I wasn't prepared for what I saw. All the roof tops were covered with bland white snow. Lawns were mountains of it. Everything was white. My driveway was a bed of ivory. Someone had shovelled it earlier in the week for the snow wasn't as high as it was on the lawn. Martin parked the car on the street and we proceeded to remove my luggage. We stepped gingerly onto crisp, crunchy snow. Ice had begun to form beneath. As my feet sank deeper and deeper into the snow drift, I had one consolation. I was wearing running shoes and not the usual high heels I love to wear when I travelled. We struggled to get to the front door. When Martin pried the screen door open, a gust of wind slapped our faces, and snow pelted our backs. By then, I was out of breath.

Once inside the warm, comfortable kitchen, I quickly plugged the kettle in for tea. Martin, realizing the predicament I was in, volunteered to shovel a path in the driveway so that I could at least, drive my car the next morning.

While the kettle boiled and Martin shovelled, I flipped through a stack of mail laying on the kitchen table. My next door neighbour had done the charitable deed again. He'd looked after the house including plants, mail, and newspapers while I was away.

My eyes were drawn to a red envelope in the stack of letters. I yanked it out of the pile, opened it, and retrieved a beautiful red, gilt-edged Valentine's card. Now, who could be sending me a Valentine's card, considering that I have no Valentine? I hadn't checked the postmark, so I opened the card to see inside.

"Hello Baby ... " it read. After the initial surprise wore off, a big grin covered my face.

He'd written me the day we said goodbye at the airport in Accra. I was planning to write him first thing in the morning.

Adamson had beaten me to the punch.

AUTHOR'S NOTE

*T*HIS MEMOIR is a work of creative nonfiction. With no plans to write a book when I travelled to West Africa, there were no notes to expand upon. Descriptions are therefore based on my memory and with the help of photographs taken. Dialogue is based on memory of actual conversations with some exaggeration for clarity and entertainment. The views and opinions expressed are my own based on observation, research and memory. No doubt other views and opinions exist about some events and places.

In order to provide anonymity for some of the characters who are still living, some of the names and titles have been changed. The book is, however, a true story based on my personal experience about an intriguing journey to West Africa.

Portions of this book have appeared in *Pride News Magazine* and the *African Connection*.

A special thanks to all my dinner guests of February 8, 1997: Jenny and Tony Aitken, Jean Brandon, Byron and Violet Carter, Mary Desousa, Gloria Wilson-Forbes, Connie Foster, Cecil Foster, Yvonne Komlenovich, Keeble and Hortense McFarlane, Errol and Emily Townshend. When I invited you all over to share my experiences after the trip, I had no plans to write a book. You are not aware of it, but it was your enthusiastic interest in the anecdotes that I shared with you and your suggestions to share the story that sowed the seed for this book. From the germination of that seed, a new dimension has been added to my life. I thank you and I love you all.

Thanks to my publisher Bill Belfontaine for his guidance and valuable suggestions, and to Karen Petherick for her most appropriate cover and book design.

A big thank you to my sister-in-law and her husband for their hospitality and added information. Sincere thanks to my dear cousin Yvonne Komlenovich for your critique. You were brutal but honest.

Thank you Bernice Lever, Sylvia Pusey, Mary Monet-Williams and Don Williams for your first gloss over and or preliminary edit of some chapters of the manuscript.

Finally I'm eternally grateful to the wonderful men I met in Ghana and Nigeria, for without your overwhelming kindness, this book would not have been written.

Reverend Suobite visited me in Toronto in 1998 and although Adamson Mone had an obsession to visit Canada, he never made it. He passed away in February 2000—I miss him terribly.

Kwame Nkrumah's statue and mausoleum.

Dual fountain at Kwame Nkrumah's memorial Park.

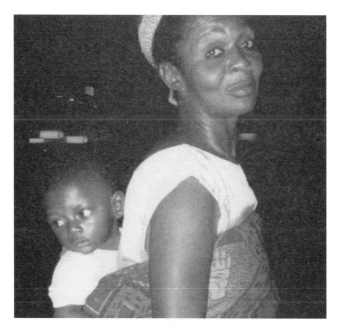

Mother and child on the street of Accra.

Awash with perspiration, I try on my first African outfit made for me by Pearl.

My first and last meeting with Paddy – outside a Chinese restaurant.

The streets of Kumasi.

The lion and the medicine man – at round-a-bout in Kumasi.

Kumasi Market

With Reverend Suobite in front of his office in Port Harcourt

The streets of Owerri – remnant of Biafran War

A campus building at University of Ksugha –
poinciana tree covered with flowers in front.

Professor Ojo and wife Mabel in their home in Jos, Nigeria

Jos Market

Boulders of Jos

A lizard crawls along the wall at University of Nigeria, Lagos.

With the banker – Mr. Ekwue in Lagos.

A B O U T T H E A U T H O R

*Y*vonne Blackwood has published several short stories and writes columns for newspapers, including the Toronto Star. She has been a banker with the Royal Bank of Canada for the past twenty-eight years. She is also the Marketing Director for the Canadian Authors Association and an active community volunteer. Yvonne was born in Jamaica and immigrated to Canada in 1976. She lives in Markham, Ontario. She has two children, Michelle and Robert and is the grandmother of Eliza and Monroe.